I0829194

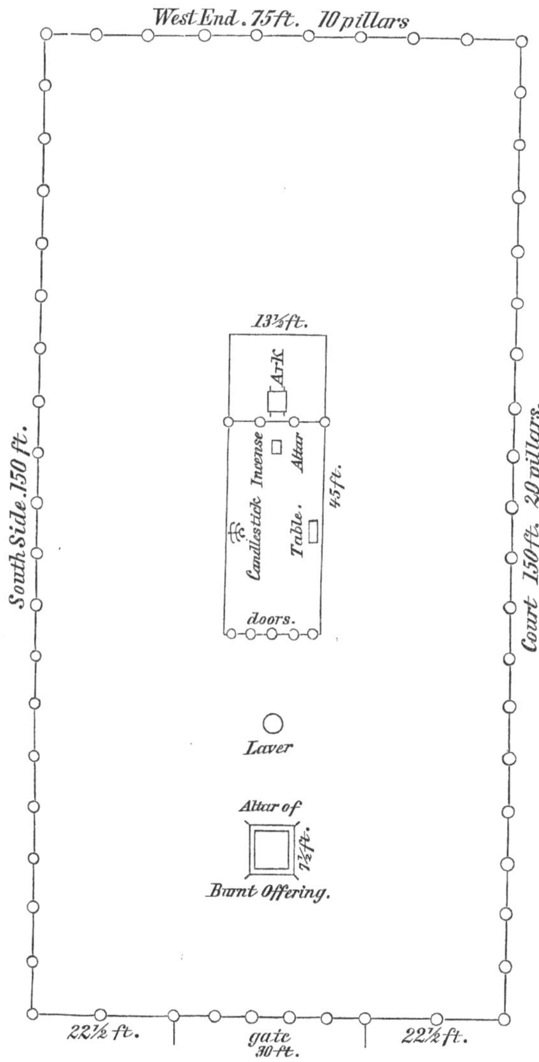
West End . 75 ft. 10 pillars
South Side . 150 ft.
Court 150 ft. 20 pillars.
13½ ft.
Ark
Incense
Altar
Candlestick
Table.
45 ft.
doors.
Laver
Altar of
7½ ft.
Burnt Offering.
22½ ft.
gate
30 ft.
22½ ft.

THE TABERNACLE,

OR

THE GOSPEL ACCORDING TO MOSES.

BY

GEORGE JUNKIN, D.D. LL.D.,

LATE PRESIDENT OF WASHINGTON COLLEGE, VIRGINIA.

PHILADELPHIA:
PRESBYTERIAN BOARD OF PUBLICATION,
No. 821 Chestnut Street.

STEREOTYPED BY WESTCOTT & THOMSON.

TO THE READER.

You have, in these chapters, gleanings from a field in which this labourer has toiled for more than half a century. Four times has he delivered the doctrines here set forth, in the form of lectures: first to his pastoral charge proper; afterwards, to the still more important charges successively, in Lafayette College, Miami University, and Washington College, Virginia. Each delivery was accompanied with a careful revision of the whole matter under consideration. Nevertheless, these are *reminiscences*, for the fortunes of war have cut him off from all his books, papers and even letter files: so that, present labour and the remembrances of fifty years back, are here presented, combined, and condensed into this little volume. The tiny book is a compend of Christian theology. I say *Christian* theology; for I have, long ago, been forced into the conviction, that without a diligent study of the tabernacle, no man ever acquires clear, transparent, and practical views of evangelical truth in systematic order. A few things you will find here, different from commonly received interpretations. Prominence is given to the central point of the moral universe; and care is taken to keep the symbols separate and distinct. My views in regard to the cherubim, which were given to the public twenty-one years ago, have been revised, by such aids as were within my reach; but no material changes from the Lectures on Prophecy have been thought necessary or proper. Reference to other men's opinions have not been made Perhaps it is due to myself and to truth, to remark, that Fairbairn's Typology I had not seen, until nearly through with these chapters, and therefore, it can scarcely be said, that *I dissent* from his opinions, even where we differ. Dr. Newton's excellent book on these subjects, had almost arrested my long cherished purpose to write out my views. After, however, reading it and finding some points of difference in minor matters, I came to Elihu's conclusion, though for a different reason, "Therefore I said, Hearken to me; I also will show mine opinion."

PHILADELPHIA, *February* 1, A.D. 1865.

CONTENTS.

CHAPTER XVIII.

CHAPTER XIX.

CHAPTER XX.

THE TABERNACLE,

OR

THE GOSPEL ACCORDING TO MOSES.

CHAPTER I.

Symbolization.

THERE is no immediate communication between the souls of men in this world. Without the instrumentalities of our bodily organs, we know nothing whatever of each other's spiritual nature, condition, or character. Indeed, our knowledge of *self*, is equally dependent on the physical organism with which our thinking substance is connected. John Locke, the greatest of modern metaphysicians, traces the commencement of our ideas to sensation and reflection. This has been by some misunderstood, at least, misapplied. But still, it is substantially true: the first knowledge we have is the immediate result of excitement in our nervous system. The history of man's creation implies, first, the formation of the wonderfully complicated material habitation for the rational spirit; then the breathing into his nostrils the breath of life. What the connection is and how it is formed between the body and the soul, we are entirely ignorant; and yet there is no knowledge more certain, than that such connection exists—that the spirit within us operates upon the body and the body influences the spirit. The mystery here lies in the manner; and is to us, thus far, inscrutable. No person doubts the fact, nor his ignorance of its mode. A man born blind and so continuing, has no knowledge of colours: the deaf has no idea of sounds; and so of all the other senses: and, were all wanting, the mind would have no ideas at all; and so could not engage in those interminable processes of reasoning, which Locke comprehends under the term *reflection.*

Now, it is this mysterious, but most intimate connection between soul and body, that unites together the two worlds—the world of matter and the world of spirit; and makes it possible for us to illustrate the one by the other. Hence the comparisons, parables, allegories of Scripture. Hence the multitudinous efforts of men, in all ages, to embody deity in visible form. Idolatry is but a perverse abuse of this natural susceptibility: a vain attempt to create a new medium of intercourse and communion between the visible and the invisible. But these abuses constitute no valid objection against symbolical representations of sacred truths; such as we have in comparisons, parables and allegories, where resemblance of relations enables us to make plain, spiritual things, by natural things more plain and easily comprehended. As all the intercourse and communion of spirit with spirit is through the medium of our physical organism; so God has been pleased to make our intercourse and communion with himself, dependent upon material media. He established a covenant with our first parent and set up the tree of life as a symbol of its blessings upon condition of his compliance. When Adam sinned and placed himself and his posterity under a dispensation of wrath, it pleased God, in his sovereign love, to reveal his dispensation of mercy and to guaranty eternal salvation to all who should believe in the promised Messiah—the seed of the woman. He thereupon instituted bloody sacrifices, as the outward sign and symbol of the cardinal truth in the glorious gospel scheme: thus creating a medium of intercourse and communion between the redeemed and the ever blessed Father: thus for ever presenting, in the burning sacrifice, the memento of the promised salvation through the death of the Saviour. This same principle we have, expanded in the whole arrangements established at Sinai; in the somewhat complicated and arbitrary, but yet significant structure of the tabernacle, its furniture, appurtenances, and the worship of which it was the centre and the medium.

In process of their exposition, it will be best to follow the order of the sacred text, as given by Moses, in his account of the construction of the furniture, the tabernacle and all its surroundings.

With the single exception of the altar of burnt-offerings, the order of the text is probably the order of importance.

As each several object is taken up, it will be most natural to give, (1) a description of the material structure; (2) then its symbolical substance, that is the doctrine which it represents: then, (3) when we shall have gone over the whole in detail, to bring them together; (4) note their relative positions severally, and in reference to the whole, as one system.

CHAPTER II.

The Ark of the Testimony.

EXOD. xxxvii. 1–9. "And Bezaleel made the ark of shittim wood: two cubits and a half was the length of it, and a cubit and a half the breadth of it, and a cubit and a half the height of it: and he overlaid it with pure gold within and without, and made a crown of gold to it round about. And he cast for it four rings of gold, *to be set* by the four corners of it; even two rings upon the one side of it and two rings upon the other side of it. And he made staves of shittim wood and overlaid them with gold. And he put the staves into the rings by the sides of the ark, to bear the ark. And he made the mercy-seat of pure gold: two cubits and a half was the length thereof and one cubit and a half the breadth thereof. And he made two cherubim of gold, beaten out of one piece made he them, on the two ends of the mercy-seat; one cherub on the one end on this side, and another cherub on the other end on that side; out of the mercy-seat made he the cherubim on the two ends thereof. And the cherubim spread out their wings on high, and covered with their wings over the mercy-seat, with their faces one to another; even to the mercy-seat-ward were the faces of the cherubim."

We have here an analysis of the ark into two parts; the chest or body—we may say, the ark proper; and the cover or lid, the mercy-seat.

First, the ark proper. Let us note the materials of which it is made—shittim wood. From all we can learn, the probability is, that this wood was the black acacia—a species of locust, which abounded in that region. The term implies a thorny tree; and as the boards of the tabernacle, which were twenty-seven inches wide, were made of the same, it must have been a tree of large growth; but of what particular species, is perhaps a question whose difficulty is inversely as its importance. Of this the chest and the staves for transportation were made. The length, taking the cubit at eighteen inches of our own measure, was forty-five inches, the width and the height, twenty-seven; the same as the breadth of the tabernacle boards.

This box or chest and the bearing staves were overlaid with gold. The crown of gold round about the upper part of the chest, was doubtless an ornamental network curving outward and forming a guard to prevent the lid or mercy-seat from slipping out of its place. Rings of gold were attached to each corner on the sides, through which the staves passed and lay continually ready for use in carrying the whole structure.

The cover was a plate of solid gold; the ends

turned up and wrought into figures called cherubim, with wings extended toward each other and their faces turned inward and downward, as if looking intently toward the contents of the chest.

These contents were the two tables of the law. The words were first uttered, in thunder tones, from the summit of the burning mountain. Exod. xx. They were afterward delivered to Moses, recorded by immediate divine power on the two tables of stone, and handed along ranks of angels. Acts vii. 53: "Who have received the law *by the disposition* (into ranks) of angels and have not kept it." These tables, prepared supernaturally—without any human agency—were broken by Moses when he came down from the mount—Exod. xxxii. 19: "And Moses' anger waxed hot, and he cast the tables out of his hands, and broke them beneath the mount." Afterwards, by divine command, Exod. xxxiv. 4, "he hewed two tables of stone like unto the first—and took in his hand the two tables of stone." In verse first the Lord says, "I will write upon these tables, the words that were in the first tables, which thou breakest." The statement in verse twenty-eighth, "And he wrote upon the tables the words of the covenant, the ten commandments," must therefore be understood of the Lord and not of Moses. And in Deut. x. 4, 5, we are told, "he (the Lord) wrote on the tables, according to the first writing, the ten commandments,—and I turned myself and came down from the mount, and put the tables in the ark which I had made; and there they be, as the Lord commanded me."

Here we have an apparent inconsistency in the Scripture statements. Paul, Heb. ix. 4, says of the ark, "wherein was the golden pot that had manna, and Aaron's rod that budded, and the tables of the covenant." But Moses said unto Aaron, Exod. xv. 33, "Take a pot, and put an omer of manna therein, and lay it up before the Lord. * * * * * * And Aaron laid it up before the testimony to be kept." And so, as to the rod, Num. xv. 10, "And the Lord said unto Moses, Bring Aaron's rod again before the testimony." These show that there was a prefix—a coffer or shelf appended at the forward end of the ark for these articles. All difficulty vanishes, if we read, instead of *wherein*, *whereupon*, or, *on which*, was the golden pot, &c. And this is allowable; and so we have, as the sole contents of the ark, the tables containing the ten commandments; and this is expressly affirmed, 1 Kings, viii. 9: "There was nothing in the ark save the two tables of stone."

CHAPTER III.

The Tables of Stone—What do they Symbolize.

THESE were made, as we have seen, before any part of the tabernacle furniture. Their history heralds forth their transcendent importance. No compend of moral truth may pretend to compare with them, for glory and grandeur of origin; for simplicity and completeness of adaptation to man's necessities; or for sublime exhibitions of the Divine perfections. Such an illustrious transcript of the moral attributes of God and his claims upon the supreme adoration of men, and of their obligations to one another, is sought for in vain among the records of human wisdom. And how should it be otherwise? Who so fit to adapt law to his creatures as their Maker? Who but Jehovah himself can reveal the perfections of his own being? Whose right is it to dictate law to the moral universe, if not its Author? But Jehovah exists as the Elohim—the plurality of persons in the essential unity. Has the issuance of these ten words any special reference to this personality? Certainly; the testimony of Jesus is the spirit of prophecy. All that man knows truly of the Divine perfections, he knows through the teachings of the second person in the Elohim—the divine Logos, by whom the world was made and without whom was not anything made that was made. It was the voice of the Word, afterwards made flesh—the same Word which said Let there be light, and there was light, that thundered from the summit of the burning mountain these ten words, and afterwards delivered them to Moses along the ranks of angels. This will be evident upon a comparison of a few scriptures. In Psal. lxviii. 17, 18, 20, we read, "The chariots of God are twenty thousand, even thousands of angels: the Lord is among them as in Sinai, in the holy place. Thou hast ascended on high, thou hast led captivity captive: thou hast received gifts for men; yea, for the rebellious also, that the Lord God might dwell among them. * * * * And unto God the Lord belong the issues from death." But now this is applied, in Eph. iv. to Christ: "When he ascended up on high he led captivity captive, and gave gifts unto men. Now that he ascended, what is it but that he also descended first into the lower parts of the earth?" Thus demonstrably plain it is, that it was the Lord God our Saviour who ascended, at a later period, from the tomb of Joseph to the throne of his glory in the heavens. He it was, the Man of Calvary, who, midst his thousands of angels, was in Sinai and dispensed this law. "The Lord came from Sinai, and rose up from Seir unto them: he shined forth from Mount Paran, and he came with ten thousands of saints: from his right hand went forth a fiery law for them. Yea, he loved the people."—Deut. xxxiii. 2. This fiery law and this burning mountain consumed no one, for it emanated from the gracious King of Zion. At the very interview in which he re-wrote it on the stones hewed out by Moses, "He passed by before him, and proclaimed The Lord, the Lord God, merciful and gracious, long-suffering and abundant in goodness and truth, keeping mercy for thousands, forgiving iniquity and transgression and sin, and that will by no means clear the guilty." The entire system of ceremonial observances is evangelical—all relate to the gospel scheme of salvation. "For unto us," says Paul, Heb. iv. 2, "was the gospel preached as well as unto them."

As to the kind of stone used, we are left even more in the dark than as to the wood, and therefore infer it to be a matter of no consequence. Only this is plain, that they were fragile, being shattered to pieces when thrown from Moses' hands. Nor have we anything specific as to their size, unless it be that Moses seems to have carried them down the mount, Exod. xxxii. 19, in his own hands, whence we may infer they were not very thick, and they could not have been more than forty-two or three inches long, and twenty-six wide.

The first suggestion of a symbolical meaning is durability. Engraving on stone intimates permanency. Job, in his sorrows, exclaims, chap. xix. 23, "Oh, that my words were now written! oh that they were printed in a book! that they were graven with an iron pen and lead in the rock for ever." Then he proceeds to express his faith in the living Redeemer and his hope in a glorious resurrection: truths these, which he wished to perpetuate for ever.

The first tables represented the law of God as written in the heart of man at his creation: or, we may say, human nature—Adam, with the law created in him. The breaking of the tables sets forth the fall of man and the utter defacement of God's law and image. The replacement of the tables by Moses, and the re-writing of the law upon them, by the power of the great Redeemer, forcibly illustrates his entire work of restoring man to the full dominion of the holy law, or, in other words, the restoration of the law to its ruling power over him; or may we not say the second Adam, the pattern of all the redeemed. Such symbolical meaning seems to rise up before us on the surface of the whole matter; and thus Paul seems to suggest, 2 Cor. iii. 2, 3, "Ye are our epistle, written in our hearts, known and read of all men: manifestly declared to be the epistle of Christ ministered by us, written not with ink, but with the Spirit of the living God; not in tables of stone, but in fleshly tables of the heart." So he speaks of "the work of the law written in their heart;" and Jeremiah says, "I will put my law in their inward parts, and write it in their hearts;" and, citing from Ezekiel, Paul, Heb. viii. 10, says, "I will put my laws into their mind, and write them, in their hearts." The bringing of man under the power of law, the protection of the law from violence and profanation, and the security of its rightful dominion, is therefore the grand idea herein set forth. All around it is encased within its golden enclosure. The casket indeed is precious, costly, and beautiful, but the jewels it contains are the priceless treasure.

In connection, however, with the remarks above, that the ceremonial observances are Gospel ordinances, it is important to distinguish them from the legal matter of the old covenant. The ten words and the various applications of their principles throughout the pentateuch, are quite different from the sacrifices, the lustrations, the incense burnings, the cities of refuge, &c. The former are *legal*, and whenever separated from the latter, become a law of works—the very covenant made with Adam. But the latter, coalescing with and qualifying and pointing out the way of fulfilling the former, transmute the whole into the new covenant, or true gospel, which was revealed to Adam before his expulsion from Paradise. The Israelites then, as nominal Christians now, by neglecting this distinction, converted the very doctrines of grace into a law of works. For example, when men affirm that the act of believing, *subjectively* considered—*i. e.*, the action of the sinner's own mind—as *his own*, is accounted to him for righteousness, and justifies him; what is this but justification by works? What, but the old covenant made with Adam? Thus the Judaizing Galatians converted, by perversion, the gospel in Moses, into a covenant of works: to refute which corruption Paul wrote them this argumentative epistle.

This highly important distinction explains an otherwise perplexing difficulty in the context from which the above quotation 2 Cor. iii. is taken. Claiming rightful authority and instrumental ability to write in their hearts a holy epistle, the apostle disavows his own *efficiency*, and imputes all the success of his mission at Corinth to "the Spirit of the living God," who only could write "in fleshly tables of the heart," even as "the finger of God" wrote the ten words on the tables of stone: "our sufficiency is of God." "The letter killeth:—The ministration of death, written and graven in stones." But how, if the gospel was preached unto the Israelites under the old covenant or dispensation of Moses, can that letter kill and be the ministration of death? The answer you have in the foregoing paragraph. The letter killeth—the law of Moses becomes a ministration of condemnation and of death, only as and because, men fix their minds on the letter and the tables, as contradistinguished from the positive, ceremonial institutions which are purely evangelical, and which only and alone are our schoolmaster—our pedagogue—to lead us unto Christ the great Teacher. I never could see how the moral law could be a child's leader,—(to translate the word pedagogue.) It is the sword of the Spirit to produce conviction of sin; but this, of itself, is not a grace, and tends not to draw the convicted toward Christ the teacher. On the contrary, the conscience convicted of sin only, shrinks away in terror and dismay, as in the first case—Adam and Eve hid themselves from God: and Peter said, "Depart from me, for I am a sinful man:" and the demons, "Art thou come to torment me before the time?" But I cannot help seeing how the gospel in the tabernacle should lead, by the smoke of its brazen altar, the light of its candlestick, the enticement of its shew bread, the odour of its incense, and brightness of its Shekinah, into the holiest of all, where the Lord our Righteousness dwelleth between the cherubim. It is only when unbelief despises all these, that the glorious gospel of the blessed God, whether preached by Moses, David, or Isaiah—by Jesus, Peter, or John—becomes a savour of death unto death: and it is only when mixed with faith, it becomes a savour of life unto life. But we must proceed to the second result of our analysis of the Ark, without which the symbol is incomplete, and must lead to the very error which makes the whole a ministration of death.

CHAPTER IV.

The Mercy-seat; its Symbolic Substance.

In chapter second we have given a description of the material structure. Our business now is with its typical meaning: and here we have a sub-analysis. Although there is but one piece of beaten—or very pure and malleable gold—yet the plate, or lid of the chest, is obviously distinguished from the cherubim; and therefore let us treat them severally.

Sec. I. It is obvious that the deposit of the tables in the body of the Ark is no guaranty of their protection and safety, so long as there is no cover to it. The precious contents are still exposed, though nearly surrounded with golden walls. But place on it this plate of solid gold, of adequate thickness, and of length and breadth fully commensurate with the chest itself, and of course with the tables within, and you complete the idea of protection and safety. What then does this shield of protection physical, represent, in the typical or symbolical substance? The answer cannot be mistaken: Jesus Christ is the protector and fulfiller of law. He only does all things well. Thus it becometh us to fulfil all righteousness. He is the Lord our righteousness. The law in him only, of all mankind, finds all its demands completely met. Universal obedience to its preceptive claims he only paid: and here we have the true idea of righteousness. The law of God is a straight line, and conformity with it is straightness or righteousness. Two aspects, however, must be noted of this fundamental idea.

1. The law prohibits certain things from being done: and it must be specially noted, that the decalogue presents law to us in the negative form chiefly; eight of the ten commandments are formal negations, yet involving substantial affirmatives. A ninth also, viz., the fourth commandment, is largely a negation. The fifth alone is purely affirmative. In this form our Redeemer fulfilled all law: he did no evil, nor was guile found in his mouth; and the wretched magistrate who handed him over to execution, washing his hands, said, "I am pure from the blood of this innocent person—take ye him and crucify him, for I find no fault in him."

2. But the divine law is not a mere negation. Eternal rewards are not held out to inaction. The servant who hid his Lord's money and returned it to him on his return home, was not rewarded for his negative inaction; but he was punished—"cast ye the unprofitable servant into outer darkness." Law is positive. It requires active exercise of all the talents bestowed, and it exhibits positive benefits as the rewards of active obedience. Thus did our

Redeemer fulfil law. The only positive word of the ten, he observed rigidly—he was obedient to his parents until he began to be about thirty years of age. Equally full and complete was his compliance with all positive requirements of law. Malignant ingenuity put forth its utmost efforts to prove against him sinful omission or commission, but in vain. He stands perfect in rectitude on the very records of the court that handed him over to the executioners. As is the Mercy-seat to the material substance of the tables, so is Christ to the moral and spiritual substance of the inscribed law.

Now it is exceedingly important to the right understanding of the fundamental doctrine of Christianity—the article of a standing church, as Luther called it, for us to bear in mind, that the tables record no penalty, but simply precepts. True it is, all command of authority implies penal sanction, in case of disobedience; and the Redeemer of lost men is under covenant engagements, voluntarily entered into, to meet the penal requirements of the divine law against those whom he redeems: but this Ark of the testimony is not the symbol representation of that idea. Another symbol is provided, as we shall see, to shadow forth the indispensable requisite. Here we have the one grand doctrine of justification set forth. Positive compliance with all the positive, actual demands of law is here most beautifully set forth. To such obedience, full and perfect, and to this alone is promised life, happiness, heaven, as a reward. Penal suffering is not meritorious of happiness, as we shall see when we come to treat of the altar of burnt-offerings. It is active holy obedience—righteousness, that God always rewards with life and blessedness: and this is the fundamental principle of the divine government. Deny this, and you lose the very conception of such government. Holy action shall be rewarded; unholy action shall be punished. But perfect holy action,—obedience to the divine law—*righteousness*, has been lost, as to all men by nature, and is nowhere to be found, but only in the divine Man: and this is passed over, legally accredited, in the scheme of salvation, to all that believe. "But now the righteousness of God without the law [the moral law as fulfilled by man] is manifested; being witnessed by the law [the ceremonial law of Moses] and the prophets; even the righteousness of God which is by faith of Jesus Christ unto all and upon all that believe; for there is no difference." Rom. iii. 21, 22; and ver. 26. "To declare at this time his righteousness: that he might be just and the justifier of him that believeth in Jesus." Thus, the Mercy-seat proclaims the fulfilment of the divine law by the gracious Mediator, and this holy and perfect obedience is imputed in law, and is set down to the benefit of all believers, as theirs for justification.

Moreover, as justification is inseparably connected with sanctification, we have this too symbolized in the Ark and its contents. As the letter of the law was re-written on the tables "by the finger of God," so is and must be its moral substance "written by the Spirit of the living God in fleshly tables of the heart." But of this we shall see more hereafter, when we come to consider the Laver and the relative position and order of the doctrines here typically represented.

SEC. II. We proceed with the cherubim. "The generic meaning of the Hebrew word cherub, the plural of which is cherubim, is not settled with certainty. Some critics refer it to an Arabic source, and infer the meaning to be *nearness*, *contiguity*,—hence, a *minister* or *servant:* and thus cherubim are the servants of God. Others deduce it from two Arabic words which signify "as" or "like to a boy." They are most probably correct who form the word from a Hebrew term that means to ride (raukab) by an interchange of two of the letters. This is the opinion of Poole. We have the original and the derived word brought into immediate connection in Ps. xviii. 10: "The Jehovah rode upon a cherub, and did fly." With a very slight modification, the word here translated, rode, is used to signify the car or vehicle of the cherub, in I Chron. xxviii. 18: "And of gold for the pattern of the *chariot* of the cherubim, that spread out their wings, and covered the Ark of the Covenant of the Lord."* We are not, however, safe in depending

* See Lec. X. and XI. of my work on Prophecy, for a more full account of this matter.

upon remote derivation for the meaning of words. Use is often arbitrary in modifying it, and therefore the safer method is to examine many instances where a word occurs, and by close inspection to ascertain what idea the writer expresses by it. Thus we make Scripture explain Scripture.

In pursuance of this method, as we cannot inspect all the cases in detail, because it would occupy too much space, and would become tedious, let us classify them and take up the more important. Thus we find four notable instances of their introduction: viz., the cherubim of Adam, of Moses, of Ezekiel, and of John. Those in the temple of Solomon belong to the Mosaic, being but an enlargement of these upon the Ark. But as progressive development characterizes God's works and his word, wisdom dictates the propriety of reversing the chronological order, so as to make the later development throw light back upon the earlier and more obscure. The first gospel was given to man in a commination addressed to his tempter, "he shall bruise thy head" —the seed of the woman shall crush the kingdom of Satan. This primitive, and obscurely expressed, gospel was gradually expanded, and more and more illustrated, until, as the Sun of Righteousness, it shone forth in effulgent splendour. So with the cherubim. Very little is said of them on their first presentation; the account before us is more full; Ezekiel gives more detail; and John comes still nearer an explicit revelation of their appearance and symbolic meaning. It will therefore be advisable to begin with John, and carry back what light we can to Ezekiel, to Moses, and to Eden.

The name cherubim is not used in Rev. iv. 6–9, but the description identifies the Zoa—the living creatures of this vision with those of Ezekiel and of Moses and the Seraphim of Isaiah. Preparatory to the description, we remark, there is no creature of God exactly answering to these. They are composite,—parts and portions of different animals being combined. Nor can we suppose the selections and combinations are merely accidental. The obvious reason of this complexity is, that no creature could furnish all the properties necessary to symbolize and set forth the requisite properties of the things signified by them. The infelicity of our translation in the word *beasts*, has been often pointed out. There is another word in the Revelation, translated properly, *beast*, because it means a wild animal that lives by destroying others—a beast of prey. But here it is simply *living ones*. As Christ says of himself, using this same word, "I am he that *liveth* and was dead and behold I am *alive* for evermore." These living creatures are placed in the space between the glorious central throne on which one sat that was to look upon like a jasper and a sardine stone: and round about the throne were four and twenty seats—thrones: "and out of the throne proceeded lightnings and thunderings and voices." The position of the four living creatures was upon the sea of glass in front of the great and glorious central throne, and the encircling four and twenty thrones, "and in the midst, *i. e.* the middle space between the throne, and within the circle of the thrones." This literal translation makes the sense clear; whilst our English text is unintelligible. "In the midst of the throne." If the four Zoa were in the midst of the throne, how can we conceive them to be "round about the throne." But on the sea of glass, in front, they stand, and within the circle *κυκλῳ* of the twenty-four thrones.

Now, having settled their position, let us inquire into their characteristics, and symbolization.

1. They are *living*, like the Master whom they serve. "I have set watchmen upon thy walls O Jerusalem, which shall never hold their peace, day nor night." (Isa. lxii. 6.) "Lo I am with you always, even to the end of the world."

2. Perpetual and universal vigilance. "They are full of eyes, before and behind." The true ministers of Christ—to cite from Lec. X. as above—have been, in all ages of the world, the depositaries of moral and religious knowledge, and the channels of its communication from God to man.

We may even lay down a broader proposition, and affirm that they have proved themselves to be the eyes of general science. Literature, science and general learning look to them as their great patrons. Where shine the beacon-lights of science that have not been kindled by the tapers of the church?

Where is the unbelieving philosopher, that does not owe even his capacity of traducing the ministers of God, to the literary instruction afforded by those very men?" Why, even the celebrated saying of Jefferson, "Eternal vigilance is the price of liberty," he borrowed from the Bible. How forcibly is this thought expressed in the symbol, "full of eyes, before and behind?" Where else did the Grecian mythology get its Argus with her hundred eyes, which Juno ultimately placed as ornaments in her peacock's tail? Of these ministers faithful and true, there are indeed sometimes counterfeits: such as Isaiah speaks of (lvi. 10.) "His watchmen are blind: they are all ignorant; they are all dumb dogs that cannot bark; sleeping, lying down, loving to slumber."

3. Another characteristic of God's ministry is courage—moral heroism. "The first Zoon was like a lion." Whenever the providence of God called for it, lion-hearted courage stood forth, to the wonder, and often to the vexation and dismay of the church's persecuting enemies. "The righteous are as bold as a lion." "Mark the intrepidity of Paul before Agripppa; on the Acropolis of Athens; amid the tossings of the tempestuous ocean; in the face of the mob at Jerusalem, at Ephesus, at Philippi. Look at Huss before the council of Constance and the pile of burning faggots: at Luther, the lion of the Reformation, * * * * where can we find a picture of greater moral sublimity than the

heroic reformer presents, as when, in the presence of the Emperor, the Roman Catholic clergy and nobility, with uplifted hand, and eye glancing toward heaven, he exclaims, "Here I stand, I cannot do otherwise. God help me, Amen." Lift your eye to the Alps, and behold Zuingle, the eagle of northern Switzerland; then let it fall upon the city at their base, and think of the Paul of the Reformation. Read Calvin's letter to Francis I. a production which, as it issued from the pen of the first scholar of his day, stands even yet among the very proudest productions of literary genius. In its onward sweep, let your vision pause upon the rugged mountains of Scotland. Listen to the splendid eulogy pronounced over the body of Knox by the Regent Morton, "There lies he who never feared the face of man," then pay the meed that is due to the dauntless reformer of North Britain. Truly does the lion's face represent the spirit of the gospel ministry.

4. The second Zoon is like a calf or ox. Patient endurance of toil is thus represented. "Much increase is by the strength of the ox." Prov. xiv. 4. By the uncomplaining endurance of her ministry is the church increased; by their slaughter is she fed. On them falls the stroke of persecution. "The blood of the martyrs is the seed of the church."

5. "The next trait to be noted is humanity. Affectionate sympathy with the sons and daughters of sorrow, is ever allowed to be a quality of God's

true and faithful servants." This is symbolized by the third Zoon, which "had a face as a man." This bespeaks also, intelligence and wisdom.

6. "The fourth living creature was like a flying eagle." This bird, aptly called the king of birds, as is the lion king of hearts, "by the elevation of his flight, and the keenness of his vision, beautifully represents that loftiness of soul, that singleness of heart, that quickness of penetration and promptness of action, which well become those men who minister in God's great name, and act as sentinels, to guard his timid flock in this wilderness world."

7. "And the four Zoa had each of them six wings about him." The angels of the churches, "the heralds of mercy to a ruined world, ought to move with rapidity." Nor would it be easy to devise a symbol of this characteristic more expressive than this. Universally is the wing employed for the purpose; and this is intensified here by the supernatural number; as if to triple the motive power and so the motion itself. The command is, "Go ye into all the world and preach the gospel to every creature."

8. "And they are full of eyes within." These set forth the high conscientiousness of the Christian ministry. "They are to be self-searching men. They are required, first of all, to examine themselves, before making a tender of their services to the Captain of salvation.

9. "They rest not day and night." This surely

does not intimate a restless, uneasy temperament, like a tiger in a cage; but simply, their incessant employment in their heavenly work, saying, "Holy, Holy, Holy, Lord God Almighty, which was, and is, and is to come." Here we learn the burden of their labours to be, the proclamation of the doctrine of the Trinity in the unity of the divine essence; for the phrase, *which was, and is, and is to come*, is really a translation of the sacred and incommunicable name JEHOVAH: and this fundamental doctrine, on which the entire edifice of gospel grace is built, is their never ceasing song. Reject this doctrine and all is gone: salvation is a dream. Retain it, expand it, build on it; and you have the entire system of evangelical truth.

Thus, we have presented in these apparitions of living things, all the leading attributes and qualifications of gospel ministers. The Zoa are, in our opinion, symbolical of that living agency by which the dispensation of mercy is carried on in the world. We have not here, indeed, the name cherubim; but we have the substantial essence of the thing; we have the slain lamb, between the Zoa and the throne; and we shall find in our retrograde movement, indubitable evidence of their identity. We shall also see, that in all cases where the cherubim are introduced, it is in connection with a *dispensation of mercy*—the issuing forth of the glad tidings of peace and salvation to lost men.

Ezekiel's vision, like John's, was seen in heaven

—"the heavens were opened and I saw visions of God." i. 1. In his first and detailed account, he does not use the word cherubim, any more than does John. But in chap. ix. he introduces the name in the singular, and in chap. x. in the plural. His description is of a complicated machine or car of triumph, and is not a little difficult to be understood. Without entering into minute detail, our purpose will be answered by a general statement and such detail only as will identify the vision as to substance, with that of John. Taking the whole in its unity, it is a car, bearing a glorious throne with "the appearance of the likeness of the glory of the Lord:" its wheels so constructed as to move, like a chair on castors, in any direction without turning. It is generally, and I believe correctly, understood to symbolize the divine providence—the machinery by which our Redeemer rules in and spreads his church: and herein it contains the substance of the great roll seen by John in the angel's hand.

But our concern is with the items which correspond with the Zoa of the apocalypse: and here we have: 1, The four living creatures; 2, They are full of eyes on their wheels round them, i. 18. So are their wings, x. 12. 3, "They four had the face of a man, and the face of a lion, on the right side: and they four had the face of an ox on the left side; they four also had the face of an eagle," i. 10. We learn, moreover, that the general form of their body was that of a man, v. 5. "And this was their appearance; they had the likeness of a man." They differ from the Zoa of John, in that "every one had four faces, and every one had four wings," v. 6. Here, as in John, is set forth the four characteristics of the faithful ministry, courage, humanity, patient endurance, and elevation of soul and purpose. They are perpetually active as well as vigilant. The brightness and effulgence—"and as the bow that is in the cloud in the day of rain, so was the appearance of the brightness round about," i. 28.

In short, it is impossible to read and compare the Old Testament and the New Testament prophets, in this matter, without reaching the conviction that, in substance, they are the same; and by consequence, symbolize and set forth a *dispensation of mercy.* Accordingly, in chap. ii., Ezekiel gives an account of his commission: "Son of man, I send thee to the children of Israel." And of this mission he gives an account which runs through his entire book.

Before we return to Moses it is proper here to note the seraphim of Isaiah. Chap. vi. 1–3: "In the year that King Uzziah died I saw also the Lord sitting upon a throne, high and lifted up, and his train filled the temple. Above it stood the seraphim; each one had six wings; with twain he covered his face, and with twain he covered his feet, and with twain he did fly. And one cried unto another and said, Holy, Holy, Holy, is the Lord of hosts: the whole earth is full of his glory."

We can hardly restrain the remark, that the visions and prophecies connected with this triumphal, wheeled car, surmounted by its brilliant throne and bow, were largely then future and are still future. The restoration of the Jews and the wars of Gog and Magog, see chap. 37, 38 and 39, are certainly yet future: "it shall be in the latter days." Hence these wheels and wings, indicating rapid movements in all directions, represent all the agencies employed by Him who sitteth on his throne. These are the days of church extension, of Bible Societies, and missions.

The word *Seraphim* signifies *burning ones*,—bright, fiery-coloured, flaming ones. Their office and wings evince their identity with the living creatures of John and Ezekiel. Jehovah is also seen upon his throne, the seat or source of power, whence proceeds the ministerial commission. Accordingly, in immediate connection with this vision, Isaiah receives that heavenly charge, which he fulfilled in such a holy manner. "Then flew one of the seraphim unto me, having a live coal in his hand, which he had taken with the tongs from off the altar, and he laid it upon my lips. Also I heard the voice of the Lord, saying, Whom shall we send and who will go for us? Then said I, Here am I, send me. And he said, Go, tell this people;" go and preach the gospel, and warn sinners to flee from the wrath to come. Here again, the cherubic symbols are exhibited in connection with the delivery of the ministerial commission.

In these three manifestations of the cherubim, they are seen in vision. There was no embodiment of them in any actual, material substances. They were simply ideal representations, made to pass before, or, as it were, into the minds of the prophets. So also was it at first with Moses. The patterns of the entire tabernacle and its furniture were exhibited to him in the mount, and so vividly and indelibly impressed upon his mind, that he could direct the construction of them all in actual material substances: "And look that thou make them after their pattern, which was showed thee in the mount." Exod. xxv. 40. This is, therefore, the only instance of an embodiment in wood, stone, gold, silver, brass, cloth, or skins, of the symbolic cherubim, and their attendant implements, used in the worship of Jehovah. Permanency and intelligibility by the people, is doubtless a prominent idea in this embodiment.

What then are the Mosaic or Sinaitic cherubim designed and adapted to set forth?

1. They spring from the mercy-seat; are a unit with it; and are upheld by it. Here are symbolized, (1.) The issuance of the messengers of salvation from the Saviour himself. "All power in heaven and earth is given unto me, go ye therefore and preach the gospel to every creature." (2.) They are of the same piece of gold; this teaches the official unity of Christ and his ministry; "That they may be one, even as we are one: I in them, and

thou in me, that they may be made perfect in one; and that the world may know that thou hast sent me, and hast loved them as thou hast loved me." (3.) Permanent and constant dependence: as the cherubim rest their weight on the mercy-seat, so ministers of the gospel depend upon Christ—"Lo, I am with you alway."

2. They have the human form and face. These proclaim the intelligence and kindly sympathies of the men who minister in holy things.

3. They have the lion-face—the courage necessary to meet and defy danger and death.

4. They have the ox-face—patient endurance of labour and toil.

5. They have the eagle-face—symbol of intelligence and lofty aims.

6. They have the wings, which spread out over the mercy-seat, and betoken their readiness and ability to waft to all the world the glad tidings, that the law has been fulfilled and justification secured to all who believe in their jewel-crowned King.

7. They have their faces turned downward to the mercy-seat and the law it covers. This indicates their chief study of these things, into which the angels desire to look.

8. Their faces are turned inward, which teaches the restrictions and limitations of that dispensation: whereas those of Ezekiel and John turn outward and in all directions; because the times referred to by their ministry are aggressive: the Sinai restrictions

of the Abrahamic covenant—that middle wall of partition is broken down and the Abrahamic covenant goes forth to make Abraham the father of many nations, the heir of the world. Thus all the essential parts of the cherubim of John and of Ezekiel are here found: and were we to run into the detail of every part—the pins, and hooks, and rings, and cups, and tongs, and snuff-dishes, &c.—about the tabernacle, we should find even more complicated variety than in Ezekiel's vision.

Now all this is intimately connected with the divine legation of Moses, which, we have seen, notwithstanding its fiery law, is pre-eminently a mission and a ministration of mercy.

One case more remains—the cherubim of Eden. Gen. iii. 24: "So he drove out the man: and he placed at the east of the garden of Eden cherubim and a flaming sword which turned every way, to keep the way of the tree of life."

Note here the brevity of the record. These imaginary beings are not described as things new and ill understood; but as if the expected readers of the history were familiar with their general appearance and uses. This was undoubtedly the fact. A knowledge of these symbols was handed down by tradition, just as the rite of sacrifices was; and the meaning of both. Adam was cotemporary with Methuselah two hundred and forty-three years; Methuselah with Shem ninety-eight years; Shem with Isaac fifty-two years; and of course within eight years of the birth of Jacob, who was one hundred and thirty years old at the descent into Egypt; which leaves but one hundred and thirty to the birth of Moses. How easy then was it to transmit a sacred religious observance to this time; and to preserve its meaning in a religious community? Adam, Methuselah, Shem, Jacob; these four could bring it down to within one hundred and fifty years of the time when Moses had arrived at manhood. Therefore it is that he presents it as a matter with which his present and prospective readers were not unacquainted. Subsequent details surely authorize their matter to be understood of the briefer statement before us.

There is a traditionary exposition of the work of the cherubim, which we feel constrained to reject. It is that they are flaming angels, set as guards to ward off and prevent man from approaching and attempting to seize upon and eat the fruit of this tree, in the vain hope of gaining life by it. Assuming that the tree was a sacrament of the covenant of works, the agency of these living creatures is to prevent men from attempting salvation by clinging to that covenant. "To this there are two or three insuperable objections. First, the word translated *keep*, never signifies to *keep off*—to drive away; but generally, if not always, to keep in safety; to protect; to defend. In Gen. ii. 15, it means, to watch, and take care of. Adam was placed in the garden "to dress it and to *keep* it."

"For I know him," says God, concerning Abraham, "that he will command his children and his household after him; and they *shall keep* the way of the Lord." Chap. xviii. 10. "Because that Abraham *kept* my charge," xxvi. 5. "I will again feed and *keep* thy flock," xxx. 31. And God said unto Laban, "*Take heed* that thou speak not to Jacob either good or bad,—that thou speak not harshly to him," xxxi. 24. Let them "lay up corn in the land of Pharaoh, and let them *keep* food in the cities," xli. 35. These are all the instances of the word's occurrence (according to Trommius) in Genesis: and they clearly show that the sense is not to *keep off*—to *drive away*—but to *preserve*. So, in the passage in question, it must mean, to keep up a knowledge of the way of life;—to instruct men how they must walk if they will enjoy life—to keep constantly in the way which leads to it,—to walk in Christ who is the way, that they may enjoy him as the life."

Second. We find no instance in the Bible where cherub or cherubim means an angel, that is, a spiritual, created being, not connected with a body.

Third. The tree of life is Christ, in communion with whom is life. The tree in the garden was a symbol of that life; and the tree of life in Ezekiel's and John's visions, clearly exhibits him as the blessedness of the souls of men: his fruit is perpetual, and his leaves for the healing of the nations. Therefore, to exclude men from him could not be the work of holy beings. See Lec. XI.

It remains only to repeat that this cherubic vision is given, in immediate connection with the first revelation of mercy—"he shall bruise thy head"—the destruction of Satan's kingdom and tyranny over man: and the means of this destruction—"thou shalt bruise his heel,"—his inferior nature shall suffer; and of this suffering, bloody sacrifices, divinely appointed at this time, are the standing and most expressive symbol.

We therefore conclude that the Ark, inclusive of the Mercy-seat, is the GRAND TYPE of the MESSIAH; as FULFILLER of *preceptive law* for lost men; as "the LORD our RIGHTEOUSNESS;" as the JUSTIFIER of all that believe in HIM.

This gives us the reason why it is called the Ark of the Testimony. The ten words are God's testimony to truth and right, and against all that is false and unrighteous. The Mediator who delivered the tables of stone to Moses is called a witness. "These things saith the Amen; the faithful and true witness," Rev. iii. 14. And in Rev. xix. 10, the angel says, "I am thy fellow-servant, and of thy brethren that have the testimony of Jesus: worship God: for the testimony of Jesus is the spirit of prophecy." And in Malachi iii., the Saviour calls himself "a swift witness against the sorcerers, and against the adulterers, and against false swearers, &c." So was he the subject of prophetic promise. "Behold, I have given him for a *witness* to the people, a leader and commander to the people," Is. lv. 4. The stones are called the testimony—"put into the Ark, the testimony"—"two tables of testimony." Consequently the Ark of the Testimony and the tabernacle of the testimony—"the tabernacle of witness" are mentioned in several places—as Num. xvii. 7, 8, and xviii. 2. In short, Christ's fulfilling the law is the highest conceivable testimony to its importance in reference to God's government and man's salvation.

CHAPTER V.

The Table for the Bread of Faces.

THIS was made of the same materials with the Ark, Exod. xxxvii. 10–16. It was thirty-six inches long, eighteen wide, and twenty-seven high. Its border of network and ornamental crown were similar to those of the Ark; as also were its rings in the four corners of the feet, and staves for transportation; and all overlaid with pure gold. "And he made the vessels which were upon the table, his dishes, and his spoons, and his bowls, and his covers to cover withal, of pure gold." On it were placed every Sabbath twelve cakes of bread. "And thou shalt take fine flour, and bake twelve cakes thereof: two tenth-deals shall be in one cake. And thou shalt set them in two rows, upon the pure table before the Lord. And thou shalt put pure frankincense upon each row, that it may be upon the bread for a memorial, even an offering made by fire, unto the Lord. Every Sabbath he shall set it (the bread) in order before the Lord continually, being taken from the children of Israel by an everlasting covenant. And it shall be Aaron's and his sons', and they shall eat it in the holy place: for it is most holy unto him of the offerings of the Lord made by fire by a perpetual statute," Lev. xxiv. 5–9. Here remark, (1) bread is the staple of life. The manna is called "bread from heaven." In the present case the bread is made of fine flour, ground between the millstones. (2) It is most likely unleavened, though the book nowhere affirms this expressly. The passover bread, and most, if not all else offered unto the Lord, was unleavened—Lev. ii. 5–11—"a meat offering (not flesh, but bread) baken in a pan, it shall be of fine flour, unleavened, part is burned for a memorial, and that which is left of the meat offering shall be Aaron's and his sons.' No meat offering, which ye shall bring unto the Lord, shall be made with leaven: for ye shall burn no leaven, nor any honey, in any offering of the Lord made by fire." And, vi. 14–17, "This is the law of the meat offering—he shall take of it his handful, of the flour of the meat offering—and shall burn it upon the altar for a sweet savour, even the memorial of it, unto the Lord. And the remainder thereof shall Aaron and his sons eat: with unleavened bread shall it be eaten in the holy place; in the court of the tabernacle of the congregation they shall eat it. It shall not be baken with leaven." It hardly admits of a doubt. The shew bread was unleavened.

(3.) It remained on the table from one Sabbath until the next; even on their journeys it was not omitted. (See Num. iv. 7.) Therefore is it called *shew bread*—bread of faces—bread continually before faces of the Lord. This renders it the more likely to be unleavened; for, in that climate where the manna remaining over night spoiled, leavened bread a week old would be sour.

(4.) The frankincense was probably placed in some of the dishes provided and was removed and burnt in the censers or on the incense altar, on the Sabbath, and will be noticed when we shall describe that article of furniture.

Let us inquire into the typical meaning of the table, its furniture and its contents.

In general, it exhibits Messiah as the bread of God, that comes down from heaven and sustains the life of the church. John vi. 35–39: "And Jesus said unto them, I am the bread of life. He that eateth of this bread shall live for ever." But particularly, (1) The wood and the gold, as throughout, symbolize the human and the divine natures in the person of Christ. (2) The sufferings of the Saviour may be alluded to in the grinding of the flour and the action of the fire in baking. (3) The Twelve cakes or loaves are the twelve tribes of Israel, for each and all of whom bread was provided. (4) The frankincense when offered expresses prayers and thanksgivings of the church. (5) The continual presence of the bread is a guarantee, that spiritual food shall never fail, but a store is perpetually on hand. (6) The exchange of the bread and the priests eating it in the holy place on the Sabbath sets forth clearly and forcibly, that abundant provision of spiritual food and nourishment which the Lord's day always brings with it to the people of his love. (7) Its exclusive appropriation to the priests intimates the limited privileges of the people; and prepares for the contrast of a later day, when they become elevated as kings and priests unto God. (8) The unleavened bread indicates the absence of any process of decay. Leaven is the first step towards dissolution, and its prohibition assuredly intimates the absence of all tendency to corruption in the Redeemer, who, even in a physical sense, saw no corruption. Does not this teach that in the sacramental supper, we ought not to use leavened bread, bread in the first stage toward utter putrefaction?

Moreover the other idea, suggested by the unleavened bread of the passover as an indication of being hastily driven out on a pilgrimage journey, is still applicable: we are travelling through a strange land toward the heavenly Canaan.

5

CHAPTER VI.

The Candlestick.

Exod. xxxvii. 17–24. "And he made the candlestick of pure gold: of beaten work made he the candlestick; his shaft, and his branch, his bowls, his knops, and his flowers, were of the same. And six branches going out of the sides thereof; three branches of the candlestick out of the one side thereof, and three branches of the candlestick out of the other side thereof: three bowls made after the fashion of almonds in one branch, a knop and a flower; and three bowls made like almonds in another branch: so throughout the six branches going out of the candlestick. And in the candlestick were four bowls made like almonds, his knops and his flowers: And a knop under two branches of the same, and a knop under two branches of the same, and a knop under two branches of the same, according to the six branches going out of it. Their knops and their branches were of the same: all of it was one beaten work of pure gold. And he made his seven lamps, and his snuffers, and his snuff-dishes, of pure gold. Of a talent of pure gold made he it, and all the vessels thereof."

This gives us a very distinct general notion of the lamp-stand. The four bowls made like almonds give the only difficulty in our conception; they are, I suppose, part of the one piece of beaten gold and so adjusted as to contain the oil: and are therefore of similar use with the two olive trees in Zechariah's vision, "which through the golden pipes empty the golden oil out of themselves." Zech. iv. 2, 12.

We have a base, and an upright shaft, and the three branches on each side suitably ornamented with knops and flowers; and each, like the main shaft, terminating in an ornamental cup or tulip-shaped receptacle for the lamp. For the 23d verse describes the lamps as entirely separate from the candlestick itself; as really so, as the other items mentioned: "He made his seven lamps, and his snuffers, and his snuff-dishes." The lamps, or burners, being separate, could easily be removed for cleansing, trimming and filling.

Our position is, that Christ, in his prophetic office, is herein typified. He communicates to us all the true knowledge of God and of eternal things, which we possess. He lights our way into the holiest of all. His "commandment is a lamp, and the law is light." He it was who said, Let there be light, and light was. "Unto you that fear my name, shall the Son of righteousness arise with healing in his wings." "This is the true light which lighteth every man that cometh into the world." "He teacheth as never man taught."

It may be said, I know, that "the seven golden candlesticks are the seven churches," Rev. i. 20; and the argument and inference may be, that here too, the candlestick is the symbol of the church: as He taught, "Ye are the light of the world." This is true, but it does not militate against the doctrine that Christ is typified by the candlestick. For all the light the church possesses and radiates is reflected from the sun. "Ye were some time darkness, but now are ye light in the Lord; walk as children of light." This is intimated in the fact that it is all pure gold: that the lamps are seven, the mystic number of perfection;—"seven lamps of fire burning before the throne, which are the seven spirits of God." Rev. v. 5. The Holy Ghost is sent and enlightens sinners, as he is the Spirit of God in Christ Jesus.

CHAPTER VII.

The Incense Altar.

EXOD. xxxvii. 25–28 : "And he made the incense altar of shittim wood : the length of it was a cubit, and the breadth of it a cubit ; it was four square ; and two cubits was the height of it ; the horns thereof were of the same. And he overlaid it with pure gold, both the top of it and the sides thereof round about, and the horns of it : also he made unto it a crown of gold round about." A little table, eighteen inches square and twice that in height, with a horn-like projection in each corner, all covered with pure gold, and the metal wrought in ornamental work around the edge, is the simple idea of the incense altar ; to which is affixed the rings ; and accompanying which are the staves for transportation. "And he made the holy anointing oil, and the pure incense of sweet spices, according to the work of the apothecary." "And Aaron shall burn thereon sweet incense every morning ; when he dresseth the lamps, he shall burn incense upon it. And when Aaron lighteth the lamps at even, he shall burn incense upon it, a perpetual incense before the Lord throughout your generations," Exod. xxx. 7, 8. "Let my prayer be set forth before thee as incense ; and the uplifting of my hands as the evening sacrifice," Psal. cxli. 2. And John's vision, Rev. viii. 3, becomes expository. "And there was given unto the angel much incense, that he should offer it with the prayers of the saints upon the golden altar which was before the throne." There is not, nor can there reasonably be, any diversity of opinion as to the symbol meaning. The perfume and smoke of the burning incense ascend, a beautiful type of the prayers and supplications of the saints ; and the altar, its censers and its implements all are a type of our Redeemer as the intercessor and advocate of his people before the divine throne. "We have an Advocate with the Father, even Jesus Christ, the righteous." Through him our supplications pass up, and by his advocacy the cries of our necessities become prevalent ; and from the Father, for his sake, come down all the blessings needed in the church.

CHAPTER VIII.

The Altar of Burnt-Offering.

THIS was a square frame of boards, seven and an half feet on the sides and four and an half high. "And he made the horns thereof on the four corners of it; the horns were of the same; and he overlaid it with brass. And he made all the vessels of the altar, the pots, and the shovels, and the basins, and the flesh-hooks, and the fire-pans: all the vessels thereof made he of brass. And he made for the altar a brazen grate of net-work, under the compass thereof, beneath unto the midst of it." Here we have no mention of net or crown work along the outer edges of the sides, as in the golden covered furniture; because the brazen grate, being separable and hanging down inside, had no need of such work to prevent its contents from falling out. Both the grate and the square frame had rings on the sides, at the corners, and their respective staves overlaid with brass, for their transportation.

The altar of burnt-offerings is the great and fearful type of Christ, as the suffering Saviour. It exhibits to our eyes "Our passover sacrificed for us." "He, through the eternal Spirit, offered himself without spot to God," Heb. ix. 14. "And hath given himself for us an offering and a sacrifice to God for a sweet smelling savour," Eph. v. 2. As the Apostle and High Priest of our profession, he had a fearful work to perform; and all that belongs to the rendering of satisfaction to penal justice for lost men, is here symbolized. "For it became him, for whom are all things, and by whom are all things, in bringing many sons unto glory, to make the Captain of their salvation perfect through sufferings," Heb. ii. 10. The burning altar, with its victim, is Jesus Christ and him crucified.

The doctrine of sacrifices has a divine origin. Very extensively, in the heathen world, has the custom prevailed of offering animals in sacrifice to their deities. A living animal, a sheep, a goat, an ox, is brought to the priest; its life is taken, and its body, in whole or part, is burned to ashes or cinders. Not unfrequently, by a terrible perversion, the victims offered were human beings. Every year, in the month of January, our own ancestors in the British Isles offered ninety-nine men in sacrifice to their imaginary gods. The natives of Mexico had such practice when discovered by the Spaniards. The nations of ancient Canaan abounded in this fearful sin—they made their own children pass through the fire unto Moloch. And God, by the mouth of Moses, legislated on this subject. Lev. xx. 2: "Whosoever he be that giveth any of his seed unto Moloch, shall surely be put to death." Nevertheless it was often done: Even as late as the reign of Manasseh, before Christ seven hundred years, this dreadful crime was perpetrated in Israel: And Manasseh "made his son pass through the fire," 2 Kings xxi. 6. How deep the depravity, how blinded the conscience, how terrible its lashes, to drive men into such enormity of crime! Now all these sacrifices were associated with the conception of rendering God propitious. But how could this be? Is it conceivable that the slaughtering of an innocent lamb and the burning of its body, or the murdering of an innocent child, should be pleasing to God, its Creator? Could reason dictate such a course? On the contrary, reason as well as revelation, condemns it. "Wherewith shall I come before the Lord, and bow myself before the high God? Shall I come before him with burnt-offerings, with calves of a year old? Will the Lord be pleased with thousands of rams, or with ten thousands of rivers of oil? Shall I give my first-born for my transgression, the fruit of my body for the sin of my soul?" Micah vi. 6, 7. If human sacrifices are abhorrent to reason and to the Author of reason, how do we account for them? If the destruction of even the dumb brute, and its unproductive consumption, is condemned by reason, whence the custom so general over the earth? Ye men! who proclaim the adequacy of reason, unaided by revelation, to guide man in the paths of holy duty, here is a problem for you. How do you account for the general prevalence of bloody sacrifices?

Reason is dumb. It remains for revelation to speak; she lifts the veil; and all is intelligible. This is a divine institution, ordained of God in paradise, for the specific purpose of holding up to view the promised seed of the woman, as the vicarious substitute, suffering in the law-place and room of lost men, that they may escape the dominion of the curse. God is the Lord of life and has supreme dominion over everything that lives. He therefore may do what he will with his own. Accordingly he appointed the sacrifice of animals, as types and representations of Christ's offering up himself a sacrifice for us. He clothed our first parents in the skins of the first sacrifices, ere they were expelled from the garden; and we find Abel bringing the firstlings of his flock and of the fat thereof, an offering to the Lord: and this, in the faith of the promised Messiah. See Heb. xi. 4.

This exposition is demonstrated in the habitual practice of the Hebrew worship. Lev. i. 4: "And he shall put his hand upon the head of the burnt-offering; and it shall be accepted for him to make atonement for him." So Lev. iii. 2, 8, 13, and iv. 4, 15, 24, 29, 33; Num. viii. 12. So, of the scape-goat. Lev. xvi. 21: "Aaron shall lay both his hands upon the head of the live goat, and confess over him all the iniquities of the children of Israel, and all their transgressions in all their sins, putting them upon the head of the goat." And thus "The Lord hath laid on him the iniquity of us all." 1 Pet.

ii. 24: "Who his own self bare our sins in his own body on the tree." "Behold the Lamb of God, which taketh away the sin of the world." "For he hath made him to be sin for us, who knew no sin; that we might be made the righteousness of God in him," 2 Cor. v. 21. "For it is not possible that the blood of bulls and of goats should take away sins," Heb. x. 4. But we are sanctified through the offering of the body of Jesus Christ once, v. 14. Thus satisfaction is rendered to divine justice—"The wages of sin is death"—and this death Jesus, as our Surety, endured for us, as a true vicarious substitute. "For Christ also hath once suffered for sins, the just for the unjust, that he might bring us to God, being put to death in the flesh, but quickened by the Spirit," 1 Pet. iii. 18. We repeat the blessed doctrine—The Altar of burnt-offering with all its implements, and all its services, represents the seed of the woman, the Lord our Redeemer, in his official character, as our High Priest offering up himself a sacrifice for our sins.

In this he is the legal head and surety of the saved sinner, on whom the curse of the law had lain. The worshipper who brings his sacrifice acknowledges his own life to be forfeited; and expresses his faith, that Christ typified by the sacrifice is substituted; that is, is recognized in law as taking his place and suffering for him. There is nothing like a change or transfer of moral character intimated. This were an idea too absurd to be believed for a moment—yea, almost too silly and wicked to be conceived. But there is a transfer of guilt, *i. e.*, of *liability to suffer punishment.* And this is the only conceivable sense in which "Christ bore our sins in his own body on the tree," the only sense in which he became a sin-offering for us. Guilt is the bond that binds the sinner to the stake for everlasting burning: Christ, in wondrous love, unlooses this cord from the sinner and binds it around himself. He dies in our place, and having said, "It is finished," the guilt of our sin is gone for ever. Hence it follows, by an inevitable necessity of logic, that our sins can never rise in the judgment against us. Justice eternally bars the possibility of this; and pardon to the believer follows: a pardon bought with blood—with blood divine: yet to the sinner, as from Christ, a perfect gratuity:—by grace ye are saved.

Thus, properly speaking, is the sinner *saved:* he is rescued from the curse; he is delivered from the wrath of God; "snatched from hell and the grave." Now, it may be well to note in closing, this is not *justification.* Another symbol—the Ark—sets forth that idea: positive righteousness, holy action, entitles to life everlasting: but the suffering of penal evil to the full only delivers the sinner from penal suffering. This we shall see more distinctly when we come to combine all these symbols into a grand unity, and to point out the relations of each to each, and to the comprehensive whole.

CHAPTER IX.

The Laver and his Foot.

THE word laver is of Latin origin, and signifies a washer, or wash-bowl, Exod. xxxviii. 8: "And he made the laver of brass, and the foot of it of brass, of the looking-glasses of the women, which assembled at the door of the tabernacle of the congregation." "And, chap. xl. 30, 31, 32, he set the laver between the tent of the congregation and the altar, and put water there, to wash withal. And Moses, and Aaron and his sons washed their hands and their feet thereat. When they went into the tent of the congregation, and when they came near unto the altar, they washed; as the Lord commanded Moses." And chap. xxx. 19–21: "For Aaron and his sons shall wash their hands and their feet thereat. When they go into the tabernacle of the congregation, they shall wash with water, that they die not: or when they come near to the altar to minister, to burn offering made by fire to the LORD. So they shall wash their hands and their feet, that they die not."

Let us note the material—"*brass*; of the looking-glasses." A strange transmutation this, looking-glasses into brass! Persons disposed to cavil at Scripture have noticed this as an absurdity: and have also alleged, to Moses' prejudice, that glass was not known in the world when he is claimed to have written—nearly fifteen centuries before Christ. But infidelity gains nothing by such petty cavils. All we have to do, in order to obviate both these supposed difficulties, is to acknowledge a slight infelicity in our English translation, and to correct it. The word translated looking-glasses, simply means *mirrors*, or *reflectors*, which were made in Moses' day of metal, of brass chiefly, though probably with a mixture of other metal. These metallic reflectors or mirrors would be made of very finely purified metal; which was therefore very suitable for the purpose of an instrument for cleansing.

It seems probable that the laver and his foot were separable. Possibly the wash-bowl was composed from the refined metal of reflectors; and its foot of a coarser material. This idea of two pieces is strengthened by the fact that no rings and staves are provided for its transportation: leaving us to infer that they were packed up with other things when the camp removed.

Nor have we any detail as to its shape, or dimensions, or ornaments. The brazen sea of Solomon was fifteen feet in diameter: and he constructed ten lavers. As extreme cleansing was required, it is not at all probable that the priests washed their hands and their feet by putting them into the bowl itself. Much more likely, there were separate smaller bowls, which were emptied after each ablution; or, it is probable "his foot" was a bason below the laver, with means of letting off the fouled water, and of letting down from the bowl above a new supply for the next person.

Further, we notice the high importance of these washings. The priest who neglected them perilled his own life; giving awful sanction to the command —"Be ye clean that bear the vessels of the Lord."

We now enquire for the symbolical meaning: and to this the answer is, Christ Jesus as the PURIFIER of his church. Among the last messages he delivered by the old prophets, was the promise of his personal advent. "But who may abide the day of his coming? And who shall stand when he appeareth? for he is like a refiner's fire, and like fuller's soap. And he shall sit as a refiner and purifier of silver: and he shall purify the sons of Levi, and purge them as gold and silver, that they may appear unto the Lord an offering in righteousness," Mal. iii. 2, 3. This mission was to display the law of God to his church, and to "give himself for it; that he might sanctify and cleanse it with the washing of water by the word; that he might present it to himself a glorious church, not having spot or wrinkle, or any such thing; but that it should be holy and without blemish," Eph. v. 25–27. And this glorious work he accomplishes "Not by works of righteousness which we have done, but according to his mercy he saved us, by the washing (we might translate it the laver) of regeneration and renewing of the Holy Ghost," Tit. iii. 5.

This purification is not from the guilt of sin—by *guilt* meaning liability to penal evil—to punishment. The burning altar is the exclusive symbol of this idea. But the laver symbolizes Jesus as the purifier—the cleanser from moral defilement. The two symbols are entirely separate and distinct, but having their proper relations.

It doubtless may occur, as an objection to our considering Christ as symbolized by the laver, that the work of sanctification belongs, in the economy of redemption, to the Holy Spirit. This is true, but it is as the Spirit of Christ; or as sent through him and at his intercession, that the third Person sanctifies the sinner. We hold and teach, that sanctification, which begins in regeneration and is continued through life and even in eternal ages, is the work of the Spirit. See Junkin on Sanctification, chap. vii. viii. ix. Still, only for the sufferings symbolized in the burning Altar and the righteousness by the Ark, could the Spirit be sent to do this work—"If I go not away, the Comforter, the Spirit, will not come unto you; but if I depart, I will send him unto you," Jno. xvi. 7. And our Lord's driving of the hucksters and brokers out of the temple indicates this reforming process. He gave much attention moreover to the priests and Levites, the scribes and Pharisees—to all engaged in teaching and administering the ordinances and executing the laws. And in the qualifications required for the apostleship, and for the higher office of evangelists, he procured a great reformation. Even the deacon's office was to be in the hands of holy men, full of the Holy Ghost and of wisdom. Thus he fulfils his own prophecy; and purifies the sons of Levi; calling into the sacred offices of the church men whom by his Spirit he has sanctified; and this, with the ulterior view of securing pure teachings and a holy administration. How sacred and solemn the warnings to ministers of the word, that, first of all, they should see well to their own conversion, as a preparation for the office: and then, for sustenance in the discharge of all official duties, their constant need of sanctifying influences. But for these, contained all in the promise, "Lo! I am with you alway, even to the end of the world," who would not exclaim, "Who is sufficient for these things?" The minister who does not continually resort to the laver will surely not be characterized by presenting unto the Lord offerings in righteousness.

CHAPTER X.

The Priesthood--The Holy Garments.

FROM the call of Abraham, while in Ur of the Chaldees, in the seventieth year of his life, until this Exodus, being four hundred and thirty years, there was no order of official priesthood in the church. The father of the faithful was unquestionably prophet, priest, and king in his own house: so likewise was it, most probably, with the other tribes and nations. The institutions of the cherubim and sacrifices; that to point out to man the way to obtain life by fulfilment of preceptive law, and to perpetuate the knowledge of that fulfilment for ever; this, to exhibit the sufferings of the woman's seed in fulfilment of penal law: the one, to proclaim justification of life; the other to teach redemption from death, by the death of the Redeemer himself. These, I say, having been given to man in paradise, with all the necessary explanations of their symbolic meaning, it is not conceivable that Adam should neglect or forget. The garments he and his wife wore must have been a very adequate memento of the covering proclaimed by the cherubim; and at the same time of the price of blood paid for their deliverance from the curse of the law. It is, therefore, no random guessing, when we affirm that our unhappy parents—nay, I recal that, for now, exercising faith in the promised seed, as they obviously do, they are again a happy pair; and as being blessed in the hopes of the great salvation, it is no random guess to affirm that they, looking for the promised seed, as they do—saying, I have found it —I have gotten a man from the Lord—would keep up the sacrificial offerings and in presence of the cherubim. After the birth of many children, and especially, after many of these had gone away from the parental abode, and were each, with their families, pursuing after their bread in the sweat of their faces, Adam must have been to them a ruling, and teaching, and worshipping head-king, prophet and priest. Accordingly, we find them assembling together for public worship: and this coming together and bringing their offerings unto the Lord was, "in process of time,"—or, at the end,—*the cutting off* of days: *i. e.*, most assuredly, on the Sabbath, the only end, heretofore mentioned. And here, we see, Cain brings a mere thank-offering—the fruit of the ground—an acknowledgement simply of fealty offered to the Lord as king: but Abel presents a living sacrifice—"The firstlings of his flock and the fat thereof: and the Lord had respect unto Abel and to his offering." This was manifested, and consisted in its miraculous, spontaneous combustion. We are not informed of Adam's officiating, or even of his being present on the occasion. But if we mark the brevity of the history and the whole nature of the case, I see not how we can avoid the opinion that he superintended and directed all the general affairs of his expanding family.

Now, as it must have been with this family, until it became so numerous, and spread over so large a space, as to render it impracticable for them to meet for worship in one place and to be managed by one superintendent; so, when they, by necessity, established new and additional places for their Sabbatic assemblages, the patriarchal head of these new tribes or nations would become the prophet, priest, and king; and they would carry along with them the laws, institutions, and forms of worship in which they had been educated. The cherubim they might not remove; but its symbolic meaning they could not avoid remembering more or less distinctly: and an altar they could erect anywhere. And this is the history of the world, in regard to prophet, priest, and king, for more than twenty-five centuries: except, perhaps, that in some nations there was an order of priesthood created, separate from the patriarchal head. Yet is it very certain that the powers of civil rule and religious influence and control were vested in the same persons. The very words, in various nations, which designate the priest's office, also express civil rule. Joseph's father-in-law was both a prince and a priest. And thus the combination continued down through all Grecian and Roman history. Priests there were in Egypt, and Greece, and Rome; but an order of priesthood limited to the natural succession of a single family is not, I apprehend, to be found in history at all; but only in Aaron's line. Melchisedech, who was very probably Shem, was an insulated priest and king of a tribe, but not one by succession in a regular line: neither father, nor mother, nor descent had he in any genealogical line of priesthood. If Shem was the Melchisedeck who met Abraham, and to whom that patriarch paid tithes as his superior, he had learned the ceremonies of the sacred service from his grandfather Methusaleh, with whom he was cotemporary for ninety-eight years.

Thus the first decisive movement in the history of the world toward the separation of things civil and worldly from things religious and spiritual, is in the Bible and in connection with the true religion. The rights and privileges and duties of men who minister in holy things are clearly defined; and so also of civil affairs. The king in Israel must keep within his own sphere, lest he meet with a breach, like the son of Abinadab, and give occasion to write on his habitation the sad memorial—Perez-Uzzah, 2 Sam. vi. 7, 8; or, as Uzziah, whom Azariah the priest withstood, saying, "It appertaineth not unto thee, Uzziah, to burn incense, but to the priests, the sons of Aaron, that are consecrated to burn incense: go out of the sanctuary;" * * * * "And Uzziah the king was a leper unto the day of his death," 2 Chron. xxvi. But this is a matter very different from a nation's ignoring God and setting religion at nought: very different from the proverb, "Religion has nothing to do with politics." If the king has no right to minister at the altar, neither has the priest a right to sit in the magistrate's seat; but both are under law, and bear their proper relations each to each, in the service of God.

The whole tribe of Levi was consecrated to religious services, or such as subserved religion. "Bring the tribe of Levi near, and present them before Aaron the priest, that they may minister unto him." "And I, behold, I have taken the Levites from among the children of Israel instead of all the first-born," Num. iii. The reason is, "Because all the first-born are mine; for on the day that I smote all the first-born in the land of Egypt, I hallowed unto me all the first-born in Israel, both man and beast: mine they shall be: I am the Lord." "Thou shalt give the Levites unto Aaron and to his sons: they are wholly given to him out of the children of Israel—to do the service of the tabernacle—to keep his charge, and the charge of the whole congregation." "And take thou unto thee Aaron thy brother, and his sons with him, from among the children of Israel, that he may minister unto me in the priest's office," Exod. xxviii. 1. As we have seen in chap. x., the business of the priest is to offer sacrifices of every variety and kind.

But all these are instructive; all the priest's works teach some important truths: "And that ye may teach the children of Israel all the statutes which the Lord hath spoken unto them by the hand of Moses," Lev. x. 11. And in the matter of the leprosy, they are directed to "do according to all that the priests the Levites shall teach you," Deut. xxiv. 8. And Mal. ii. 7: "For the priests' lips should keep knowledge, and they should seek the law at his mouth: for he is the messenger of the Lord of hosts."

As to the various sacrifices, it is not consistent with our plan, nor with the example of Paul, to go into much detail; and what we do will come up, when we enter upon our composition of the various particulars into one complete system. We proceed with

The holy garments. "Thou shalt make holy garments for Aaron thy brother, for glory and for beauty. And these are the garments which they shall make: a breastplate, and an ephod, and a robe, and a broidered coat, a mitre and a girdle," Exod. xxviii. 2–4. These now in the order of this text—afterwards reversing this order.

1. The *breast plate* consists of a ground work of fine twined linen, doubled, and about eight inches square. "Four square shall it be, being doubled; a span shall be the length thereof, and a span shall be the breadth thereof." Upon this foundation is wrought elegant embroidery of gold, of blue, and of purple, and of scarlet—"the gold they did beat into

thin plates, and cut it into wires." Upon or inserted into this "cunning work" are settings of stones, even four rows of stones: the first row shall be a sardius, or cornelian, a topaz, and a carbuncle. And the second row shall be an emerald, a sapphire, and a diamond. And the third row a ligure, an agate, and an amethyst; and the fourth row a beryl, an onyx, and a jasper: they shall be set in gold in their inclosings," Exod. xxviii. 15–20. These gems are of various colours, under the same names, so that we cannot know with certainty what particular hue each had; or whether variegated; and of course, to attempt an exhibition of the tribal character from the colour and value of the stone on which the name is written, would be fanciful and probably pursuing the metaphor too far. It might be entertaining, if not useful, to present a table, giving the name of the tribe, the name of the gem on which it is engraven, and the probable colour; and leave the reader to study out the history of each, with Jacob's and Moses' farewell descriptions—a good Bible lesson perhaps and an exercise in natural science:

	TRIBES.	GEMS.	COLOUR.
1	Reuben,	Sardius,	Deep red—venous blood.
	Simeon,	Cornelian, Topaz,	Brownish red—venous blood, buffy.
	Levi,	Carbuncle,	Pale red-scarlet—arterial blood.
2	Judah,	Emerald,	Bright green—foliage of spring.
	Zebulon,	Sapphire,	Blue—the sky, cloudless.
	Issachar,	Diamond,	Clear, transparent—purity.
3	Dan,	Ligure,	Yellowish green—autumn.
	Gad,	Agate,	Clouded—mossy—striped.
	Asher,	Amethyst,	Blue, violet, shading off—sky.

	TRIBES.	GEMS.	COLOUR.
4	Naphtali,	Beryl,	Pale grayish green—sea.
	Joseph,	Onyx, Chalcedony,	Variegated—striped.
	Benjamin,	Jasper,	Colours various—brown, yellow, white.

Whilst the reader may amuse, and entertain, or perhaps, instruct himself, in studying these materials of the jeweller and the lapidary in learning the language of gems and applying it to the patriarchs and their tribes respectively, we may, with certainty deduce this lesson from the breastplate, viz. : that in the use of the jewels it puts forth the high estimate the Lord sets upon the tribes of Israel, whose *memorial* is placed on the breast of the high priest, to intimate God's perpetual remembrance of his church. Besides, from their being called, the URIM and THUMMIM, the lights and perfections, it is obvious to infer, that the high priest was to be a centre from which light, learning, knowledge, should radiate, and moral perfections be diffused and cherished among the twelve tribes. And, although we know not the manner of their communication, yet it is plain from Ezra ii. 63, and Nehemiah vii. 65, that Israel was in the habit of seeking divine directions in the use of these contents of the breastplate. A question arose as to the right of the descendants of Barzillai the Gileadite, to the priesthood. Upon searching the records their names were not found. "And the Tirshatha said unto them, that they should not eat of the most holy things, till there stood up a priest with Urim and with Thummim."

In the ends of this breastplate were two rings and chains by which it was to be fastened to the other parts of the dress. Ver. 22, 23: "And thou shalt make upon the breastplate chains at the ends of wreathen work of pure gold. And thou shalt make upon the breastplate two rings of gold, and shalt put the two rings on the two ends of the breastplate." The chains were attached to the rings and the other ends of them to ouches or eyelet holes in the shoulder pieces of the ephod.

Ephod is a Hebrew word which signifies a thing *bound*—firmly attached. Our translators thought best to adopt instead of translating it. It might be rendered a *bodice*, a waistcoat, a vest, or spencer; being a garment whose base or ground was fine twined linen, on which were elegant embroidery or cunning work "of gold, blue, and purple, and scarlet." Exod. xxxix. 4, 5: "They made shoulder pieces for it, to couple it together; by the two edges was it coupled together. And the curious girdle of his ephod, that was upon it, was of the same, according to the work thereof." Ver. 6: "And they wrought onyx stones—a species of chalcedony—enclosed in ouches or settings of gold, graven, as signets are graven, with the names of the children of Israel. And he put them on the shoulders of the ephod, that they should be stones for a memorial to the children of Israel." "Six of their names on one stone, and the other six names of the rest on the other stone, according to their birth." These were connected by the two wreathen chains of gold respectively, with the upper corners of the breastplate; the lower part being bound with a lace of blue, passing through eyelet holes or ouches of gold, to the girdle; which seems to have passed over the body of the ephod, binding firmly and receiving the bands which fastened the lower edge of the breastplate. All these, viz., the ephod or bodice, the girdle, the breastplate and the shoulder pieces, including the engraved onyx stones, seems to be included sometimes under the name ephod. This article of dress thus becomes the chief and distinctive garment of the high priest.

The next, passing inward, is the *robe* of the ephod. "And thou shalt make the robe of the ephod, all of blue," Exod. xxviii. 31. "And there was a hole in the midst of the robe, as the hole of an habergeon, with a band round about the hole, that it should not rend," xxxix. 2, 3, &c. This was ornamented upon the hems, or skirts, with golden bells, and pomegranates of blue scarlet and linen. "And it shall be upon Aaron to minister; and his sound shall be heard when he goeth in unto the holy place before the Lord; and when he cometh out, that he die not."

"The broidered coat was of fine twined linen," not probably different from those made for Aaron's sons, except in the matter of the embroidering. Ver. 27 and xxviii. 4, 39, 40 and 42: "And thou shalt make linen breeches to cover their nakedness, from the loins even unto the thighs they shall reach."

The mitre or head dress of Aaron was also made of fine linen. "And they made the plate of the holy crown of pure gold, and wrote upon it a writing, like to the engravings of a signet, HOLINESS TO THE LORD," xxxix. 30, 31. "And they tied unto it a lace of blue, to fasten it on high on the mitre."

The symbolic meaning of the high priest's dress stands out pretty prominently. We have noted the items, following for the most part, the order of Moses' description. Let us now reverse this order and begin at the very body of the man himself. (1) He must be free from defect, or deformity, either natural or from being maimed and deprived of any faculty or member common to man. (2) He must be washed with water at the Laver, before he can be arrayed in his pontifical dress. This bespeaks the same truth with the golden plate of the mitre; purity; not consecration merely, or dedication to sacred use; but purity, actual freedom from all defilement in a moral respect. "Be ye clean that bear the vessels of the Lord."

(3) The same is taught by the fine, white linen, that forms the basis of all the garments except the ephod. The Levite singers at the dedication of the first temple, were "arrayed in white linen," 2 Chron. v. 12. And the fine linen, in Rev. xix. 8, clean and white—is "the righteousness of saints." This linen tunic or under garment, reached from the neck to the ancles, as was the custom in all the

eastern world; we are not informed what parts of it were embroidered: no doubt the sleeves and the part, which extended below the robe of blue, were gorgeously ornamented. Thus holiness and beauty —the beauty of holiness shone forth.

(4) Next comes the robe of blue, which reached probably from the neck to or below the knees, and which with its golden bells and artificial pomegranates may remind us of the blue heavens above us and the fruitful earth beneath, of which the robe bears the richest mineral and vegetable products.

(5) The ephod, with its curious embroidered girdle, its breastplate of judgment—its Urim and Thummim, with the names of the twelve tribes thereon and also on the two shoulder pieces, bespeaks the solemn dedication of the tribes, who are the church, to the service of God: the light the knowledge, the beauty, the glory of the Apostle and High Priest of our profession. The mitre or crown proclaims the grand end of all the doings, the teachings, the worship of the church, to be the glory of God.

(6) The high priest, thus fully and richly enrobed, is an official type of Jesus—God manifest in the flesh, in all the fulness of his qualifications for the work his Father sent him to accomplish.

CHAPTER XI.

The Tabernacle, and its Court.

It will promote perspicuity, in our description, if we attend first to the more solid parts—the frame-work of the building. And the materials must be looked into: they are wood, brass, silver, and gold. "And he made boards for the tabernacle, of shittim wood, standing. The length of a board was ten cubits—probably fifteen feet; and the breadth of a board one cubit and a half—twenty-seven inches." (See Exod. xxxvi. 20, &c.) Each board had two tenons at one end. "Thus did he make for all the boards of the tabernacle: twenty boards for the south side, southward: and forty sockets of silver he made under the twenty boards." Of course, at the cubit of eighteen inches, this determines the length of the building to be forty-five feet. The two sockets under each board were driven into the ground and the boards erected, placing the tenons in the sockets. The same number of boards and sockets were required for the north side. "And for the side—or end—of the tabernacle westward he made six boards"—which determines the width of the building to be thirteen and a half feet. For the east end "two boards were made for the corners." "And they were coupled beneath, and coupled together at the head thereof, to one ring: thus he did to both of them in both the corners." These corner boards, facing the east, thus constituted a brace and support to the sides north and south; whilst they became door-jambs, of eighteen inches, leaving the door or gateway into the building, ten feet and a half wide. "And he overlaid the boards with gold, and made their rings of gold, to be places for the bars, and overlaid the bars with gold." These bars he made of shittim wood; five for the boards on the sides north and south and five for the boards on the west end. The side bars, except the middle one, appear not to have extended the whole length of the tabernacle, for it is said "he made the middle bar to shoot through the boards, *i. e.* the rings of the boards from the one end to the other."

This building is divided into two apartments by a vail, placed across it, probably—(for the record does not determine this)—one third of the distance from the western end. Four wooden pillars, overlaid with gold and resting on sockets of silver support this vail. A similar provision is made for the door, except that the pillars are five in number and must have been placed one at each side in close connection with the corner boards; which would leave but two and a half feet for each of the four doors. These pillars were overlaid with gold and had golden fillets or rings at their chapiters or ornamental heads: "but their five sockets were of brass."

Thus, we have the frame of a building—an upright structure, three sides closed and compacted, the fourth partly open, with its five pillars, and a row of four pillars dividing off about one third of it, at the west end; all presenting an exterior of burnished, glittering gold. We have, as yet no roof; and can nowhere find in the record, any account at all of a floor.

Let us now proceed with the less solid, but not less significant parts of it: and let us follow Moses: beginning within, and working outward. And here, we may remark as to the materials, it is probable the prohibition, Exod. xxxvi. 5–7, has especial reference to these: "The people bring much more than enough for the service of the work, which the Lord commanded to make. And Moses gave commandment, and they caused it to be proclaimed throughout the camp, saying, Let neither man nor woman make any more work for the offering of the sanctuary. So the people were restrained from bringing. For the stuff they had was sufficient for all the work to make it, and too much."

The inner curtains were made of fine twined linen; this was the ground upon which were wrought cherubim of blue and purple and scarlet. Of these curtains there were ten, all alike in size and workmanship: being twenty-eight cubits—forty-two feet long, and four cubits—six feet wide. Five of these were fastened together by fifty loops of blue in the edges or selvidge; and so of the other five; (see chap. xxvi. 5, 6,) and thus we have two immense curtains or sheets of embroidered linen, each forty-two feet by thirty; and when these two are united by the taches of gold, and they become "one tabernacle," it is sixty feet by forty-two.

Now, if this large cloth be suspended by hooks hanging nine inches below the upper ends of the boards all round, it will constitute the lining of the walls on the two sides and the west end, and become a ceiling: for the length of the building is forty-five, and the height of it fifteen, making sixty the precise length of the two sets of curtains, when clasped together by the fifty golden taches: and the two sides equal thirty feet, to which add the width, and you have forty-three and a half; whereas the curtains, severally, before their attachment, were forty-two feet long. Thus we stand within a chamber forty-five by thirteen and a half feet, and fifteen high; and we behold nothing but the beautiful white linen, ornamented with cherubim of blue, and purple, and scarlet. The partition we have not yet erected. This is constructed of the same material, except that the blue seems to be the ground. Chap. xxvi. 31: "Thou shalt make a vail of blue, and purple, scarlet, and fine twined linen of cunning work: with cherubim shall it be made. And thou shalt hang it upon four pillars of shittim wood overlaid with gold: their hooks shall be of gold, upon the four sockets of silver." And, ver. 36, "Thou shalt make a hanging for the door of the tent, of blue, and purple, and scarlet, and fine twined linen, wrought with needle-work."

We have already mentioned the omission of any flooring for the tent. Two other items of seeming necessity are wanting in the description, and left to be suggested by their necessity: viz., a cross-tie on the eastern end, at the top; and some support to the roof, to prevent the heavy outer coverings from sagging down and forming a dish-like cavity, in which rain would lodge, to the great inconvenience and detriment of the whole building and its furniture. How this was effected, and of what material, we are not informed; but some upbearers there must have been, to form a pediment or slope to the roof. And this will appear as we proceed with the outside coverings, which are three.

The first is composed of hair-cloth. Exod. xxvi. 7–13: "And thou shalt make curtains of goats' hair to be a covering upon the tabernacle: eleven curtains shalt thou make." Their length thirty cubits, forty-five feet; their breadth four cubits, six feet. They are coupled together, five in one sheet and six in the other; and these two great sections are coupled together by fifty taches or clasps of brass. Then the whole is laid over the building outside, as were the linen curtains hung inside; except that the additional sixth or eleventh curtain is folded half over or under its other half—"and shalt double the sixth curtain in the fore front of the tabernacle." This gives strength and binds it the more firmly. From "the fore front," along the top, to the west end is forty-five feet; add fifteen feet from there to the lower ends of the boards, and you have sixty feet: *i. e.*, six feet less than the curtains when all attached into one. Of this surplus three feet are taken up by the fold just mentioned; and, ver. 12, the other three are folded in like manner at the bottom next the ground. From the lower ends of the boards over the top to the lower ends on the other side is forty-three and a half feet: but the hair-cloth curtains are forty-five feet. This surplus cubit appears to be divided, so as to reach nine inches below the boards "on this side and on that side, to cover it." Thus we have a black tent, such, for colour and texture, as are seen in that country to the present time: the gold being completely enveloped and concealed; inside by the linen embroidered curtain, outside by the goats' hair-cloth.

Besides this, there were two other coverings over the Ark. xxxvi. 19: "And he made a covering for the tent of rams' skins dyed red; and a covering of badgers' skins above that." The rams' skins, or, as we would now call them, the morocco leather covering, must have been composed of many pieces firmly sewed together. So also must the badgers' skins, this animal being smaller than the other.

Both these covers are for utility, and not for ornament. What animal was meant by the word rendered badger, is not certainly determined: nor is it our business, at least it is not indispensable for our present purpose to inquire. The uses to which these skins were applied evince their nature. In the days of Ezekiel, nearly nine hundred years later, we find a reference to them, chap. xvi. 10: he reminds Israel of these very times of sojourn and the low depression of the nation, and their helpless estate: "I clothed thee also with broidered work, and shod thee with badgers' skin," &c. These, therefore, made a thick and strong leather, impervious to rain, and suitable for shoes. So in Num. iv. 10–14, the priests are directed to pack up the candlestick and all its appurtenances, the incense altar, and all the instruments of ministry, and "put them in a cloth of blue," and "the censer, the flesh-hooks, and the shovels, and the basins, and all the vessels of the altar—in a purple cloth;" all, after being thus covered with cloth, are to be covered with a covering of badger skins. This makes it evident what was the character of these skins, and of the leather made of them, if indeed it was dressed at all.

The size of these two coverings is not given; and the mode of attaching them to the building is left for us to imagine. From their obvious use, we imagine they extended simply upon the top and a short distance beyond, so as to form a suitable eave, to throw the water off the tent all round.

Before we enquire into the symbolic meaning of this structure, let us construct "the court of the tabernacle." This was an enclosure of one hundred cubits by fifty—one hundred and fifty feet by seventy-five. Like the tabernacle, the longer sides of this parallelogram extended east and west, and the gate faced the east. "The hangings of the court were of fine twined linen, a hundred cubits: their pillars were twenty, and their brazen sockets twenty; the hooks of the pillars and their fillets were of silver," Exod. xxxviii. 9, 10. The pillars themselves of brass, xxxvii. 10, 11. The height of this curtain wall of fine white linen was five cubits, seven and a half feet. "And for the gate of the court shall be a hanging of twenty cubits, of blue, and purple, and scarlet, and fine twined linen, wrought with needle-work: and their pillars shall be four and their sockets four," xxvii. 16. Thus, we have an enclosure of one hundred and fifty feet by seventy-five: the three sides, north, south, and west, shut in by white linen curtains, seven and a half feet in height, suspended by silver hooks and fillets upon fifty pillars of brass, set in sockets of brass, and their capitals overlaid with silver: the remaining, or eastern, side is enclosed in the same manner, except that an opening of twenty cubits, or thirty feet, in the centre is left for a gateway; whilst the fifteen cubits on each side of it are shut up with the white linen. What was the character of the needle-work which distinguished the gate curtain we are not expressly informed; but the high presumption is, that it was the same as the interior curtains of the tabernacle; viz., cherubim.

CHAPTER XII.

The Symbolic Meaning of the Tabernacle and its Court.

THE general symbolic meaning of the tabernacle and its court was THE CHURCH OF GOD. The tabernacle, with all that appertains thereunto, is a visible type of the visible kingdom of our Lord upon earth. As related to time, it is divided into three dispensations, the patriarchal, the Mosaic, and the Messianic. The patriarchal dispensation extends from the first revelation of mercy—the *proto-euangellion*, given to Adam in paradise, to this organization under Moses ; being two thousand five hundred and eight years. The Mosaic, from this period, A. M. 2508, to Pentecost A. D. 34, a duration of one thousand five hundred and twenty-six years. The Messianic period of the church extends from A. D. 34, until the second personal advent; its precise limit and duration are known only to the King himself. "But the saints of the Most High shall take the kingdom, and possess the kingdom for ever, even for ever and ever," Dan. vii. 18.

Two proofs—rather clases of proofs of this are presented. The former is the suitableness or adaptation of these entire structures and arrangements to typify the church. And here note,

I. The court is the larger space of the enclosure; and that into which is the wider entrance; though we have no express statement to that amount, it is almost certain, the common people were permitted to enter it. Certainly the offerer of a living sacrifice was allowed to enter, for he must bring his offering to the priest at the altar and there lay his hand on its head. And in John's vision, Rev. xi. 2, he is directed to leave the court out, for the reason, that it is to be trodden under foot. This refers to a period then future; but it shows that the court, as was that of the temple, is less pure and sacred than the other enclosures—an idea plainly inferable from its flimsy material—its inferiority as to expense and beauty, and its being uncovered. All this suits it to represent the less organized and more loose and undefined religious observances of the first period, during which there was no official priesthood, nor any specified ordinances of divine service. The necessity of a suffering Redeemer, as exhibited in the altar; and the necessity of purification, as set forth by the laver (both of which are in the court) this early church had. But it lacked many advantages guaranteed in the second.

2. The Cherubim—the well-known types of the messengers of mercy—on the curtains of the gate, constitute a standing invitation to the outer world, to enter in and engage in the true worship of the true God.

3. The smoke and flame of the burning altar,

which were possessed by the church from the beginning, are here suited to express the faith of the worshippers, in the promised Messiah; and also to call the nations to dedicate themselves to God.

II. The holy place into which the priests only were permitted to enter, represents the Mosaic economy—an advanced position. Here the ministering priests are surrounded on all sides by the golden walls; and the cherubim of glory, on the pure and fine twined linen, constantly remind them of that purity symbolized by the laver, at which they must wash before their entrance, and of their obligations to bear on more than angelic wings, to a lost world, the message of salvation by the blood of the sacrificed lamb; without offering of which they themselves cannot enter. Here they have the light of the candlestick—the light of the world—to guide their feet in the path of duty. Here they have the bread of heaven to nourish and nerve them up to the solemn and important duties of their office of ministering between the living and the dead; and of bringing the world to bow at the feet of Messiah.

Here, too, they have the incense from the altar, reminding them of our Advocate with the Father; and thereby pointing to a still holier and more glorious state of the church yet future; into which she shall enter, when the middle wall of partition shall be removed and the vail be rent; this signifying, that the way is open into the holiest of all.

III. The most holy apartment of this building, is therefore by itself well adapted to typify the gospel church, with its newly-fledged and swift-winged ministry; its higher measure of purity; its fuller and clearer exhibitions of the mercy which covers the law and proclaims its perfect fulfilment; whilst the atonement thereon made, shows the efficacy of the great sacrifice for sin; and the consequent pardon of all who flee to the Rock of Ages for protection in obedience, by the fulfilment of law, both preceptive and penal, consummates the work of Messiah and promises the extension of its glorious benefits over the whole earth. This spread of the kingdom is exhibited by the double symbols—the cherubim on the walls and ceilings; and by those of gold on the mercy-seat.

We proceed to the second class of proofs, that the tabernacle symbolizes the church, viz. direct Scripture testimony. And (1) when God gave directions for building this tent, he said, "Let them make me a sanctuary; that I may dwell among them," Exod. xxv. 8. "And I will dwell among the children of Israel and will be their God," Exod. xxix. 45. "I the Lord dwell among the children of Israel," Num. xxxv. 34: (See Ps. ix. 11: cxxxv. 21: lxxx. 1: lxxxvi. 2.) (2) Jacob said, after his vision of the ladder, "This is none other but the house of God, and this is the gate of heaven," Gen. xxviii. 17. Wherever God makes himself known to the souls of his people, that is his house. "But will God in very deed dwell with men on the earth? Behold, heaven, and the heaven of heavens cannot contain thee, how much less this house which I have built?" 1 Chron. vi. 18. The tabernacle is often called the house of God. Josh. ix. 23: Jud. xx. 18, 26, 31: and so is the temple continually. (3) He has established the bright, shining glory as the token and evidence of his presence: the pillar of fire, the glory in the tabernacle and especially above the mercy-seat; and the same in the temple at its dedication, are tokens of the divine presence in the church. But this material dwelling was the type of that spiritual temple of lively stones which is erecting to the praise of his glorious grace. "And are built upon the foundation of the apostles and prophets, Jesus Christ himself being the chief corner-stone; in whom all the building fitly framed together groweth unto a holy temple in the Lord; in whom ye also are builded together for an habitation of God through the Spirit," Eph. ii. 20–22. "For ye are the temple of the living God; as God hath said, I will dwell in them, and walk in them; and I will be their God and they shall be my people," 2 Cor. vi. 16. This is quoted from Ex. xxix. 4, 5, 6, where the purpose of these constructions is stated. And Lev. xxvi. 12, "And I will walk among you and will be your God, and ye shall be my people." There can be no doubt; the church of God is ONE. "And Moses verily was faithful in all his house as a servant, for a testimony of those things which were to be spoken after; but Christ as a Son over his own house; whose house are we, if we hold fast the confidence and the rejoicing of the hope firm unto the end," Heb. iii. 5, 6.

There is also, obvious reference to these decorations in that beautiful Scripture, the xlv. Psalm: "The king's daughter is all glorious within: her clothing is of wrought gold. She shall be brought unto the king in raiment of needle-work." Externally, like her divine Lord, she may appear as a root out of a dry ground—like a rough Arabian tent in the wilderness; but internally, her moral beauty, excellence and glory, command the admiration of all holy beings, and the angels of glory desire to look upon her and minister to her wants.

This house of God, in which he desires to dwell, this church of the living God in which he has dwelt from the days of Eden, must detain us yet a little. An important enquiry must be met, before we proceed to the collocation of the items discussed and explained, and the composition of the whole into one system.

Is this the visible or the invisible church? "The catholic or universal church, which is invisible, consists of the whole number of the elect, that have been, are, or shall be gathered into one, under Christ, the head thereof; and is the spouse, the body, the fulness of him that filleth all in all," Confession, chap. xxv. It is called *invisible* because its members cannot be certainly designated or segregated and known of men, as an organized body, bound together by visible bonds and distinguishable from the rest of mankind. But, "The visible church, which is also catholic or universal under the gospel, (not confined to one nation as before under the law,) consists of all those throughout the world, that profess the true religion, together with their children; and is the kingdom of the Lord Jesus Christ, the house and family of God, out of which there is no ordinary possibility of salvation," Confession, xxv. This distinction is well made, for it exists in the Scriptures, and did exist in fact before any part of them was written. "According as he hath chosen us in him before the foundation of the world, that we should be holy and without blame before him in love," Eph. i. 4. Plainly, all who shall be found on Christ's right hand, at the judgment, and none others, belong to the church invisible. To affirm therefore, that there is no salvation out of the church—if you mean this body that is not on earth visible—is, to repeat a truism, the saved are the saved, the elect are the elect. But most unhappily, sometimes, this assertion is made of the church that is visible, and of course, under this twofold meaning and application of the term *church*, a most grievous and uncharitable falsehood is set forth. Our Confession avoids this by the guarded language "out of which"—meaning *outside of*, unconnected with which—"there is no ordinary possibility of salvation." This excludes non-professors, unbaptized children, and heathen; and decides nothing in their cases. Salvation is ordinarily within the visible church: those that ultimately reach heaven, the elect, are ordinarily gathered within the range of the means of grace and offers of salvation.

God was never without witness to his truth as expressed in the law given to man at his creation, and in the gospel made known to him in paradise. There were always public testifiers, and testimonies, and visible ordinances of divine service. But the very brief history of the first two thousand and seventy-eight years, leaves us very much in the dark as to details. Sacrifices we know and the cherubic figures, or their memorial history, continued throughout that period, whose whole history, and chronology, and political geography, including the flood, is contained in eleven brief chapters. Yet, it was not until the call of Abram, A. M. 2078, and the covenant made with him, that the church, as far as we know, can properly be said to have been organized; since that the visible ordinances pre-existent, continued and were confirmed by an external seal of membership; and with a range comprehensive of all the nations of the world. This covenant with Abraham perpetuates all and everything like public ordinances, and guarantees its own universality; and these, under the sign and seal of the righteousness of faith—faith in the promised Messiah, which promise is limited to his seed.

From Abraham's call and covenant until the exodus and the Sinai covenant—a period of four hundred and thirty years—his family constituted a visible, social body, a people separated and segregated: and their history leaves no room for the question, whether this was the visible or the invisible church. At Sinai there was a modification of the ecclesiastical covenant, not a withdrawal certainly, of any spiritual privileges inherited by this people from Abraham, but a restriction of its blessings to this favoured family. We have the formality of its construction in Exod. xix. 3, &c.: "Moses went up unto God, and the Lord called unto him out of the mountain, saying, Thus shalt thou say to the house of Jacob, and tell the children of Israel: Ye have seen what I did unto the Egyptians, and how I bare you on eagles' wings and brought you unto myself. Now therefore, if ye will obey my voice indeed, and keep my covenant, then ye shall be a peculiar treasure unto me above all people, for all the earth is mine: And ye shall be unto me a kingdom of priests and a holy nation. These are the words which ye shall speak unto the children of Israel. And Moses came and called for the elders of the people, and laid before their faces all these words which the Lord commanded him. And all the people answered together and said: All that the Lord hath spoken we will do. And Moses returned the words of the people unto the Lord." This is re-stated by Moses. Deut. v. 2: "The Lord our God made a covenant with us in Horeb." And he proceeds in verse seventh, &c., to recite the ten commands, as an essential part of the covenant, and, accordingly, they are repeatedly called the "tables of the covenant," Deut. ix. 9, 14, 15. And the Israelites are often designated his "peculiar people"—his "peculiar treasure." So long as they should continue faithful to their covenant engagements, they should continue his peculiar people, and the blessings of the Abrahamic covenant were restricted to them. This is the law that was added because of transgressions, Gal. iii. 19. Accordingly when Israel transgressed the covenant by rejecting the promised Messiah, their covenant of peculiar restrictions was prostrated, the middle wall of partition was broken down, and the covenant of Abraham came into operation, in all its length and breadth; and the casting away of the Jews became "the reconciling of the world." See Rom. xi. Indubitably this covenant, with all its vast increase of outward, visible establishments, beyond the more simple observance of the Abrahamic institutions, relate to the church visible; and the only sense in which this visible church is *catholic*, that is, *universal*, is that quoted above from the Confession of Faith, chap. xxv., viz.: "not confined to one nation as before under the law." All people, in all the nations, who profess the true religion, together with their children, belong to the visible kingdom of our Lord; in them he dwells as in his tabernacle of old: and this is the living habitation on earth, of the living God, symbolized by the tabernacle of witness built at Sinai, according to the pattern shown to Moses in the holy mount.

One other proof, that the church visible is typified by the tabernacle and its court, is the fact that all the other symbolic representations are included within it. Every great doctrine of salvation is taught by its typical furniture: and thus it harmonizes with the declaration of our Confession—or rather, the declaration harmonizes with it—that "out of it there is no ordinary possibility of salvation." Salvation cometh by faith, and faith cometh by hearing: but how can they hear without a preacher? and how can they preach unless they be sent? Out of Zion shall go forth the law and the word of the Lord from Jerusalem. The angels of mercy, on cherubic wings, fly all abroad, proclaiming peace on earth; good will to men.

CHAPTER XIII.

The Putting Up and the Taking Down.

"AND it came to pass in the first month in the second year, on the first day of the month, that the tabernacle was reared up." This was Anno Mundi 2509, and of course Ante Christum 1491.

The work is said to have been done by Moses, undoubtedly in the same sense that the manufacture and building was done by him, *i. e.*, through the agents whom God qualified and Moses directed in everything. The first move is of course to set in the ground the silver sockets at the proper distances —"and fasten his sockets, and set up the boards thereof, and put in the bars thereof, and rear up his pillars." Thus the framework is compacted together, Exod. xl. There is no express mention made of the suspension of the great linen curtain that lines the interior; neither in the directions nor in the execution. It is doubtless included in the general statement, that "he put the covering of the tent above upon it;" although this seems to refer to the outside covering of hair-cloth; and the leathern roofs are named; and also the vail of partition and the door curtains. "And he took and put the testimony into the Ark, and set the staves on the Ark; and put the Mercy-seat above upon the Ark; and he brought the Ark into the tabernacle, and set up the vail of the covering; and covered the Ark of the Testimony"—that is, closed it in with the vail, suspended perpendicularly from its own proper pillars.

The table he set without the vail, in the larger apartment, on the north side; and placed the bread thereon, as commanded.

The candlestick he set opposite the table on the south side, and lighted the lamps before the Lord; as the Lord commanded Moses.

"And he put the golden altar in the tent of the congregation, before the vail; and he burnt sweet incense thereon; as the Lord commanded Moses."

Thus the whole interior is furnished. "And he put the altar of burnt-offering by the door of the tabernacle of the tent of the congregation, and offered upon it the burnt-offering and the meat-offering; as the Lord commanded Moses. Between the altar and the door of the tent, he placed the laver and put water therein." "And he reared up the court round about the tabernacle and the altar, and set up the hanging of the court gate. So Moses finished the work."

Thus far, the erection; let us for a moment mark the contrary service. The record is in Num. iv. 5–15: "When the camp setteth forward, Aaron shall come, and his sons, and they shall take down the covering vail, and cover the Ark of Testimony with it. And shall put thereon the covering of badgers' skins, and shall spread over it a cloth wholly of blue, and shall put in the stones thereof." Doubtless the blue cloth was spread first, or at least second, over the vail and under the skins; as in all the other cases—the table, the candlestick, the golden altar, and even the altar of burnt-offering—in all instances the outside covers are of badgers' skins. The table is something peculiar—"And upon the table of shew bread they shall spread a cloth of blue, and put thereon the dishes, and the spoons, and the bowls, and the covers to cover withal, and the continual bread shall be thereon:" —the blue seems to have been spread on top of the twelve loaves; then the vessels, and then "they shall spread upon them a cloth of scarlet, and cover the same with a covering of badgers' skins." The candlestick and its lamps, tongs, snuff-dishes, &c., and the incense altar, are covered with blue cloth and skins as before, and the bars adjusted for transportation. Of the laver no special mention is made: it may be included in the package described in ver. 12: "all the instruments of ministry," &c., which were packed in the same method and attached to a bar.

The brazen altar differs from the other articles in that the cloth is to be purple: and no mention is made of its separation into the two parts, as described in Exod. xxxviii. The frame, or stand, and the grate are both supplied with rings and staves; and in transportation were no doubt carried separately. Probably the laver was among the vessels thereof, packed in the grated basin for transportation.

When this operation of packing is finished, the Kohathites, descendants of the second son of Levi, are introduced as the bearers of these most precious articles—"After that, the sons of Kohath shall come to bear it; but they shall not touch any holy thing, lest they die. These things are the burden of the sons of Kohath in the tabernacle of the congregation." So in ver. 20: "They shall not go in to see when the holy things are covered, lest they die." For this reason none of the covered wagons presented by the princes "were given to the sons of Kohath: because the service of the sanctuary belonging unto them was that they should bear upon their shoulders," chap. vii. 9. The Gershonites—see chap. iv. 24–26—were charged with the transportation of the lighter and less sacred parts; the curtains, and all the covers of the tabernacle and of the court. To them were assigned two wagons and four oxen, vii. 7: whilst to the sons of Merari, the third son of Levi, were assigned the boards, the bars, the pillars, sockets, pins, &c., of the tabernacle and the court, iv. 29–33: and they had four wagons and eight oxen, vii. 8, and iii. 36–37.

CHAPTER XIV.

The Cloud of Glory--Pillar of Fire.

God is light, and in him is no darkness at all. Light is sweet, and a pleasant thing it is for the eyes to behold the sun. Nevertheless, intense, excessive brightness overpowers our organs of vision and causes pain; and, if continued, destroys the organ itself. So Moses found it, when he set up the tabernacle. "Then a cloud covered the tent of the congregation, and the glory of the Lord filled the tabernacle. And Moses was not able to enter into the tent of the congregation, because the cloud abode thereon, and the glory of the Lord filled the tabernacle," Exod. xl. 34, 35. So, at the dedication of the temple—1 Kings, viii. 10, 11—"The priests could not stand to minister because of the cloud; for the glory of the Lord had filled the house of the Lord." Our English word *glory*, derived from the Latin *gloria*, through the French, expresses, simply and originally, a bright, shining light. But we have almost ceased to use it in the original sense, and constantly employ it in the secondary meaning, as the symbol of *displayed excellence;* and that either intellectual or moral, or both combined. Whenever high qualities are displayed, we ascribe glory to the individual: and the highest manifestations of excellence call forth the exclamation and ascription of "Glory to God in the highest." There is, therefore, a manifest impropriety in the distinction sometimes made or intended by the phrases, "the essential glory," and "the declarative glory of God." If *glory* is the shining forth of excellence, it must necessarily be declarative, and only declarative, and the use of this as a qualifying epithet is tautological. Glory is the declaration of excellence.

Moses first saw this in the burning bush on Mount Horeb. "And the angel of the Lord appeared unto him in a flame of fire out of the midst of a bush: and he looked, and, behold, the bush burned with fire, and the bush was not consumed, Exod. iii. 2–4. This bush typified the church of God, then enduring hardness, in the midst of the brick-kilns of Egypt. But amid these fires of persecution, now as always, the Lord dwelleth in her. The non-consumption of the bush exhibits the power of Him that dwelleth therein, to save her, as on a subsequent occasion the same Angel saved his three friends in the midst of the burning fiery furnace. Of course, this is no created, but the uncreated Angel Redeemer: and Moses hid his face; for he was afraid to look upon God." Here was no form or visible figure of God; for when Moses, Exod. xxxiii. 18–20, said, "I beseech thee, shew me thy glory;" the Lord said, "Thou canst not see my face; for there shall no man see me and live." The bright light, like a burning flame, was the whole appearance: and this is the standing symbol of God's gracious presence; or, we may say, *this non-consuming fire, was a sign and token of the present Mediator.* Never was it exhibited, but in connection with a dispensation of mercy. As conducting a dispensation of wrath, the same glorious personage "is a consuming fire." "The Lord thy God is he which goeth before thee; as a consuming fire thou shalt destroy them," Deut. ix. 3. In this there is a beautiful and philosophical significance; the light and the heat of natural fire are distinct and separable. Light does not consume; heat does. Light typifies God our Redeemer, in whom justice and mercy meet together in the salvation of his people; the heat, the fire has spent its force on the humanity, which he offered up a burnt-offering for his people. But his consuming heat accompanies the light of his justice, in all the fires of his indignation and wrath upon the workers of iniquity. The Sun of righteousness hath healing in his wings, only "to you that fear his name: but all the proud, yea, and all that do wickedly, shall be stubble: and the day that cometh shall burn them up."

We hope our reader is convinced, that the cherubim of Eden, of Sinai, of Chebar, and of Patmos, and the seraphim of Isaiah, are all one and the self-same symbol; and that they, being always exhibited in connection with a ministration of mercy, are types of the entire living agency, which Messiah employs to communicate glad tidings to lost men. If this hope is well founded, may we not, dear reader, rise to a full assurance of hope, that the bright light—the Shekinah of Adam; of Moses at the bush, at the Red Sea, on the summit of Sinai, between the cherubim over the mercy-seat, above the tent; of Solomon at the dedication; of Ezekiel throughout his visions; and of John in Patmos; you will be convinced are one and the self-same symbol of God's presence in the church, whence he dispenses his mercy to lost men? In this hope we remark,

1. There was, in all these instances a bright light, distinct from the cherubim; though constantly accompanying them whenever they appeared. In Gen. iii. 24, it is called "a flaming sword which turned every way to guard the way of the tree of life." In the bush, we have the light only—a brilliant flame, and so at the Red Sea. In the tabernacle, where the cherubim are embodied, the Shekinah is distinct and hovered over the cherubim and the ark. So at the dedication of the temple, the glory shone forth from the ark, and filled the whole building. In Ezek. i. 4, it is "a fire infolding itself;" and in x. 4, 19, "The glory of the Lord went up from the cherub—and the house was filled with the cloud."

2. The forms assumed by this bright light vary.

At Eden, as we translate, it is "a flaming sword which turned every way." In Walton's Polyglot, there is considerable variety of translation; but all implying a bright, fiery appearance moving in curve lines or circles: and in Ezekiel i. 4, though the words differ, the conception suggested is the same," "a fire infolding itself," or as in the margin, "catching itself," a vast circular flame. Now, a circle being the natural symbol of eternity, we have here an eternal light, a glory without beginning or end: and out of this circle of glory, proceeds "the likeness of four living creatures"—the grand types of the ministers of mercy.

In the bush at Horeb, this non-consuming fire is not described, as to form; but "God called unto him out of the midst of the bush." This is the voice of mercy, as in Ezekiel's non-consuming fire infolding itself.

3. As before stated, the glory at Sinai, where God the Redeemer was in the midst of his chariots, twenty thousand—even thousands of angels, Ps. lxviii.; yet no specific form was presented; and the reason was given; viz. lest afterwards the people should make an image and fall into idolatrous practices: "For ye saw no manner of similitude on the day that the LORD spake unto you in Horeb out of the midst of the fire; Lest ye corrupt yourselves, and make you a graven image, the similitude of any figure," Deut. iv. 15, 16.

4. The form, of a pillar of a cloud by day and

of fire by night, accompanied the Israelites during their entire journeyings, from Succoth to Canaan. This was not however a figure of any animal or natural object; but simply a column rising and floating as it were, in the atmosphere, Exod. xiii. 21, 22, and xiv. 19, 20: and Num. x. 34, 35, 36, "And the cloud of the Lord was upon them by day, when they went out of the camp. And it came to pass, when the ark set forward, that Moses said, Rise up LORD and let thine enemies be scattered; and let them that hate thee flee before thee. And when it rested, he said, Return, O LORD, unto the many thousands of Israel."

5. The same is true, as to the other three appearances of the Shekinah, or *established* light. At the dedication of the tabernacle and the temple, and in the visions of Ezekiel, we have the brilliant light—the non-consuming fire, distinct from the material cherubim in the two first, and the imagery in the last. In John's vision, there is a large addition to all other appearances, except perhaps, Ezekiel's. Still we have the Zoa separate from all the brilliant lights. All these displays exhibit that true Light, which lighteth every man that cometh into the world.

CHAPTER XV.

Farther Symbolic Significance of the two Preceding Chapters.

WITH all reasonable caution against seeking fanciful analogies, and running into too minute details, we hope the following will be admitted, as legitimate suggestions, arising from the matter of chapters xiii. and xiv.

1. The organization of the church is accomplished by the agencies of God's own appointment. Aaron and his sons and other Levites, no doubt, were employed by Moses, in the first erection; for neither the priests, nor the furniture of the tabernacle, were as yet formally consecrated with the holy anointing oil. But afterwards, when the pillar of the cloud had removed, the most sacred things were handled only by the priests; and other parts of the holy things, by other Levites in their order. Thus, all the spiritual arrangements toward the public services in the church, were then and are now committed to the various officers, duly called into her service. "And no man taketh this honour unto himself, but he that is called of God, as was Aaron." As there were very many and very various materials worked into parts of the building and its furniture,

and every part and portion, however small and apparently insignificant, was necessary in its proper place, so in the spiritual house, there are officers and servants of all grades necessary, and each one has his proper place and duty. It is greatly to be feared that public sentiment in the church of our day and country has swung over from that excess, even to superstition, of reverence for the sacred offices indulged in other days and countries, to the opposite extreme. The officers of the church do not command the respect and exercise the influence due to the office. But be this as it may, the collecting of the materials for the spiritual temple, and their arrangement and collocation in its sacred walls, is the proper work of the missionaries symbolized by the cherubim, and the priesthood and Levitical services. "For we are labourers together with God: ye are God's husbandry, ye are God's building." "Know ye not that ye are the temple of God? and that the Spirit of God dwelleth in you?" Let the men, who aspire to minister in holy things, see to it that they are themselves sprinkled with atoning blood, and anointed with that divine unction set forth in the holy anointing oil, so shall they build upon the chief corner-stone. Therefore,

2. These builders and these carriers are under very special orders and are to act with great solemnity. As Moses was commanded to put off his shoes because the place whereon he stood was holy ground, and as the sons of Kohath were not allowed even to

look upon the ark which they were appointed to carry, so Isaiah, lii. 7–12, speaklng of the gospel day, exclaims, "How beautiful upon the mountains are the feet of him that bringeth good tidings, that publisheth peace;" and enjoins, "Be ye clean that bear the vessels of the Lord." Men that minister in holy things should themselves be holy. Mere official consecration is easily distinguishable from personal purity, and alas! easily separable from it. Such separation in fact, is doubtless often the antecedent of that want of respect just alluded to. It is scarcely possible, even for godly men, to exercise respectful regard toward ministers who have only official consecration, but fail to give evidence of personal piety. Even a few such melancholy cases have a pernicious influence, and are seized upon by the ungodly world, to which they in truth belong, as grounds of disparagement to the whole ministry and the church. To such traducers we would say, wherefore all this reproach to the church and her ministry? The church does not profess omniscience in herself, nor perfect holiness in her public servants. She does what she can toward searching men's hearts who are called into her ministry, that she may have only holy hands to be lifted up without wrath and doubting. But considering the imperfection of her knowledge and the depths of Satan's cunning as he dwells in the hearts of the children of this world, it is no marvel if, occasionally, one of yourselves succeeds in deceiving her and finding your way into her ministry as did a Judas among the twelve. But, even could you succeed in one out of twelve, and thrust your man upon us, contrary to our rules and to the dictates of a sound conscience, what is this to glory over? Is it not to glory in your own shame? Who is the more reprehensible? Whose cheek should be the more deeply mantled with the blush of shame—the deceiver or the deceived? "Cursed be the deceiver which hath in his flock a male, and voweth, and sacrificeth unto the Lord a corrupt thing."

3. May we not learn a lesson from the place of this re-organization? Holy ground is found in the desert of Arabia. The ark and tabernacle are constructed on the very borders of a great and howling wilderness, into which it at once plunged and seemed lost among the wild and barren sands. Does not this physical relation, beautifully and forcibly, point out the spiritual relationship of the true visible church, in the midst of an ungodly world? All that is in the world, the lust of the flesh, the lust of the eyes, and the pride of life, is not of the Father, but is of the world. How then should the sanctified of God find their life and enjoyment in such a barren wild? If ye were of the world, the world would love his own; but because ye are not of the world, but I have chosen you out of the world, therefore the world hateth you. And this suggests another remark.

4. Divine guidance is indispensable. The Sheki-

nah must lead; that is the church must always follow the God of mercy. These are they which follow the Lamb whithersoever he goeth. So it was in an earlier day. Abraham left his country and his kindred at the call of God, and went out, not knowing whither he went. He simply trusted in God, and, watching the tokens of his providence, and hearkening to the voice of his word, commenced the pilgrimage of a long and a happy life. A hundred and five years he wandered, a sojourner in a strange land, although it was his by covenant and sure to be his in possession by his seed. Here we have no continuing city, but following, not a supernatural light of a cloud and pillar of fire, but the more sure word of prophecy, the people of God now and ever press onward toward that glorious city, beyond this wilderness world, whose Maker and Builder is God. The commandment is a lamp and the law is light; and the path of the just shineth more and more unto the perfect day. Let it evermore be our concern to seek unto this true Light, so shall we be guided and kept by the power of God through faith unto salvation.

Sustenance from God is guaranteed. He sends none on a warfare at his own charges; but provides all necessary good things. In the thirty-nine years' travel they lacked not bread or clothing. This sets forth the abundant and perpetual supply of grace to Zion's travellers through this barren desert. The righteous man shall dwell on high, his place of defence shall be the munitions of rocks, bread shall be given him, his water shall be sure. "I will abundantly bless her provision: I will satisfy her poor with bread. I will also clothe her priests with salvation: and her saints shall shout aloud for joy." "They shall hunger no more, neither thirst; the sun shall not smite them; for he that hath mercy on them shall lead them, even by the springs of water shall he guide them. I am the bread of life: he that cometh to me shall never hunger; and he that believeth on me shall never thirst."

CHAPTER XVI.

The Holy Anointing Oil--The Consecration of the Tabernacle and its Furniture, and of the Priesthood.

MOSES was directed—Exod. xxx. 23, &c.—"Take thou also unto thee, principal spices, of pure myrrh five hundred shekels, and of sweet cinnamon half so much, even two hundred and fifty shekels, and of sweet calamus two hundred and fifty shekels; and of cassia five hundred shekels, after the shekel of the sanctuary; and of oil olive a hin: and thou shalt make it an oil of holy ointment, an ointment compounded after the art of the apothecary: it shall be a holy anointing oil."

The workmanship reveals the character and attributes of the workman. "I will praise thee," says the psalmist, "for I am fearfully and wonderfully made." Even limiting ourselves to the physical organism, this is most reasonable: and in our material structure, no part is more wonderful than the nervous systems: for whichever we look into, we are soon met with unsolvable problems. What is the relation of the different systems—or parts of the one grand system? How do the sentient and involuntary nerves operate? Are they telegraphic wires? How does the spirit influence the nerves of motion? How do the respiratory nerves keep up the proper action of the vital functions independently on mental action and consciousness? How do sensations run along these infinitesimal wires; and upon reaching their grand centre, how do they act upon the sentient mind? Such questions teach us our ignorance. Still, we see many uses of these mysterious facts; and our ignorance of modes does not cut us off from innumerable and very happy results. The child in years and the child in knowledge are made happy by beholding the beauty of the rose, the lily, and the dahlia; and by inhaling the odour of the myrrh, the cinnamon, the calamus, and the cassia. The olfactory nerves are also sentinels. Placed, in animal economy generally, in very near proximity to the gate by which the materials must enter for the support of life, they stand ever ready to give warning and enter their protest against unwholesome food. Odours acting on these infinitely fine ramifications of this nerve, serve as direct and positive means of happiness; and also as prophylactic remedies against evils. On the theory that odours are effluvia, or small particles emanating from the odorous body and drawn into contact with the olfactory nerves, we see how inconceivably minute those particles must be. The vase once saturated with them continues to send them forth for thousands of years; and yet no perceptible diminution of its bulk or weight has been detected.

Thus we have practically an idea of infinity; and that an infinity of felicities: and here is the philosophy of the holy anointing oil or unguent. It is the symbol of the Holy Ghost, as the Generator of life eternal in the soul, and of all its graces and felicities in time and in eternity.

There is another compound of sweet spices, described in this chapter, ver. 34–38, which is not an ointment, but simply a perfume. It consists of equal parts, as we translate, of "stacte, and onycha, and galbanum—with pure frankincense—and thou shalt make it a perfume, a confection." "Part of it is to be laid up, and put before the testimony in the tabernacle of the congregation." That these are distinct is evident from their composition, the ingredients of each excluding the other; and accordingly they are for different uses. Both are composed of sweet spices; the ointment, for application to things and men; the perfume, to be placed beside the pot of manna in front of the Ark, and to be offered in the censer and on the golden Altar. This is the more sacred and holy; though, in regard of both, the prohibition against their use for any but the purposes explicitly set forth, is full and express: "Whosoever compoundeth any like it (the ointment,) or whosoever putteth any of it upon a stranger, shall even be cut off from his people," ver. 33. "Whosoever shall make like unto that to smell thereto, shall be cut off from his people," ver. 38. Suspension or excommunication is the censure for each or either offence. Their diversity or distinctness seems plainly intimated, when the collection of materials is ordered. Exod. xxv. 6: "Oil for the light, spices for anointing oil, and for sweet incense." The sacredness of both is seen in the prohibition and penalty. The sweet incense is the prayers of the saints ascending through the agency of our High Priest, and perfumed with his intercession. "Let my prayer be set forth before thee as incense; and the lifting up of my hands as the evening sacrifice," Ps. cxli. 2.

The holy anointing oil is the Spirit of grace and the Spirit of office, descending upon the person or thing consecrated to the service of God.

The order to consecrate the tabernacle, and its furniture, and the priests, we have in this same thirtieth chapter of Exodus; the detail of its ceremonies in Lev. viii. And the first thing to be observed is its publicity. "And Moses did as the Lord commanded him; and the assembly was gathered together unto the door of the tabernacle of the congregation," ver. 4. Doubtless the chief of the elders and principal or leading men out of the respective tribes were present to witness the sacred inauguration. The entire mass, of course, could not be present, so as to hear and sec the grand ceremonies. The people were nearly three millions in number, and the only sense in which they could possibly be assembled at the tabernacle door, was by delegation. We learn from this, that the people should be present and express their acquiescence in the ordination of their spiritual rulers and teachers. The matter of the transaction is substantially a covenant, and the parties to it should meet face to face.

2. The next step is the ceremony of purification: "And Moses brought Aaron and his sons, and washed them with water." The laver stood before the door of the tabernacle, and between it and the altar. The extent of this operation—whether the entire person was washed or only their hands and their feet, is not absolutely determined. The latter is the more probable opinion. It seems to be supported by Exod. xxx. 19–21: "And Aaron and his sons shall wash their hands and their feet thereat." "So they shall wash their hands and their feet." And xl. 31, 32: "And Moses and Aaron and his sons washed their feet thereat—when they came near unto the altar they washed." So, at the last passover, when Peter, on second thought, expressed the desire to be washed from head to foot, Christ said, "He that is washed needeth not save to wash his feet, but is clean every whit." It is therefore most probable that this lustration was limited to the hands and feet, and not of the whole body, which would scarcely comport with the decencies of so public an assemblage. The symbolic meaning of this process is unmistakable: purity, moral purity, in the ministry of mercy is the prominent idea. And, as to Aaron, as a typical officer,

its antitype is found in John's washing Jesus on the occasion of his entrance upon the functions of the High Priest's office.

The 3d step in this process of consecration is the clothing of Aaron in the entire suit prepared, as described in chapter tenth. These splendid and costly garments, these official robes and decorations, these Urim and Thummim, these precious gems and golden crown, being after all but carnal and "beggarly elements," yet typify and set forth the inimitable grandeur and glory of our High Priest. Earth's richest materials are thrown together and wrought into the most elegant forms, by heaven-inspired artizans, for the embellishment of the priest who ministers at the earthly altars and the worldly sanctuary; and all this to impress the mind of the church with the transcendent grandeur and glory of Him who is to come from heaven and minister in the spiritual tabernacle, and to build up his own spiritual temple, to the glory of his own grace. We dwell not here, because, by reference to chap. x. the reader will see in detail the symbolic meaning of every part of this dress and the unity of its design.

4. The fourth movement is the anointing of the dedicated things. Lev. viii. 10: "And Moses took the anointing oil, and anointed the tabernacle and all that was therein, and sanctified them. And he sprinkled thereof upon the altar seven times, and anointed the altar and all his vessels, both the laver

and his foot, to sanctify them." The seven sprinklings of the altar are designed to arrest and fix attention upon it. Seven, being a mystic number, which means perfection, an abundant sufficiency, impresses the minds of the Israelites with the supreme importance of the altar: *i. e.*, the thing symbolized by it, viz., Christ our sacrifice. Thus are they taught the sevenfold importance of this fundamental doctrine, the vicarious sufferings of Jesus—his enduring the wrath of God due to us for sin.

The laver and its foot are here mentioned as being outside, and in some sort as an appendage to the altar; intimating its use as preparatory to entrance. Moreover, this seems to confirm the remark made relative to its transportation in connection with the grate of the altar.

In regard to each item of furniture, this anointing teaches the specific consecration of Christ to that particular department of the Mediatorial work symbolized by that particular furniture. And so of the

5th. "And he poured of the anointing oil upon Aaron's head, and anointed him, to sanctify him." As he is an official type of our true and efficient High Priest, his personal consecration prominently sets forth Christ's entire consecration to the office to which he was called, as was Aaron: and also his endowment and qualification by the Spirit's being poured out upon him without measure. "God, thy

God, hath anointed thee with the oil of gladness above thy fellows. All thy garments smell of myrrh, and aloes, and cassia, out of the ivory palaces, whereby they have made thee glad," Ps. xlv. And "God giveth not the Spirit by measure unto him," Jno. iii. 34. "For it pleased the Father that in Him should all fulness dwell," Col. i. 19. "For in Him dwelleth all the fulness of the godhead bodily," ii. 9. And of him ultimately is that written, "I have found David my servant; with my holy oil have I anointed him," Ps. lxxxix. 20. In short, all the qualifications of the God-man, for the work of salvation, are covered and sealed by this holy anointing.

6. One more item only, consisting of three parts, shall I mention, the sacrifices for purifying the altar, the sin-offering, the burnt-offering, and the ram of consecration. Upon the head of each Aaron and his sons laid their hands, indicative of a transfer of guilt. They are all slain, and their blood variously applied. Of the first, it was put upon the horns of the altar round about, and the rest of the blood was poured out at the bottom of the altar; of the second, the blood was sprinkled in like manner, and parts of the body were burnt. Of the ram of consecration, Moses took part of the blood and put it upon the tip of Aaron's right ear, and upon the thumb of his right hand, and upon the great toe of his right foot; it was also sprinkled upon the altar, and upon the ears, thumbs, and toes of his sons;

and parts of the flesh, along with cakes of unleavened bread, after being placed on the hands of Aaron and his sons, and waved for a wave-offering before the Lord, were burnt upon the altar.

More minuteness of detail is not consistent with our plan. These leading items afford a practical type of Christ's entire consecration, dedication, and preparation for the entire work of redeeming lost men, and glorifying God in their salvation.

CHAPTER XVII.

The Relations of the Truths Symbolized to each other and to the Grand System—The Shekinah—The Central Doctrine of Christianity.

We come now to the fifth and last result of our analysis, viz., to point out the position of the several doctrines symbolized relatively to each other and to the whole as one system. The importance of this will develope itself as we progress; yet it may be well to remark, that, as a duty out of place becomes a sin, so a truth out of place becomes a delusion and a falsehood. "To obey is better than sacrifice, and to hearken than the fat of rams;" yet the sinner who labours at obedience to the law, in hope of life thereby, seeking "to establish his own righteousness," sins against God and his own soul; and thus also converts the truth of God into a lie. For there is not, nor can be, any holy obedience until the heart is made holy—no pure water until the fountain is purified. He that cometh to God must come in the way of his appointment, or he will certainly meet the stern rebuke, "Who hath required this at your hand, to tread my courts?—bring no more vain oblations; incense is an abomination unto me." "If thou bring thy gift to the altar, and there rememberest that thy brother hath aught against thee, leave there thy gift before the altar, and go thy way; first be reconciled to thy brother, and then come and offer thy gift," Matt. v. 23, 24. Otherwise the offering is a vain oblation and a sin.

The traveller in the Arabian desert, oppressed by the scorching heat of the sun, direct and reflected from the parched sands, and his eyes almost blinded by the combined action of both, his bosom heaving with the swelling desire, Oh that some shadow of a great rock in this weary land, or even of some friendly tree, would extend its protection over me and snatch me from this impending death, at last lifts his weary and bedimmed eyes, when lo! in the distance a cloud bigger than a man's hand, seems to throw itself up in the western horizon. Toward it he bends his weary steps, hoping for its shady protection and refreshing shower. Faint, yet pursuing, he presses on, and as he nears it, it seems to rise from the earth and to culminate in the very heavens. Painfully apprehensive that night may cast its dark shade over him in this dread wilderness, he glances his eye toward the fast descending sun, and doubles his diligence to escape before the blackness of darkness covers his path. But alas! too late; in darkness and despair he sinks to the earth in a swoon: but in a moment he rallies, and what do his eyes behold? The cloud has passed away, to which he had so eagerly looked for relief, when lo! the darkness has indeed passed away, "but a light from heaven, above the brightness of the sun, shining round about" him, guides his footsteps in the same direction; and as it is a light without any scorching heat, he arises and presses onward, renewedly anxious to learn what he may about this non-consuming pillar of fire. Soon he discovers at its base other objects of interest, of which anon. He finds himself in the vicinity of a vast encampment—thousands of tents spread out in beautiful order, covering millions of peaceful, happy, and contented people. Passing the sentinels inward toward this brilliant light, he finds its base resting upon the largest and loftiest of the tents; it stands in the centre of the vast camp. Upon enquiry he learns that in this large tent is an ark containing the compend of moral law; that covering this ark is a plate of solid gold; that there are upon it, and over it, and of it, two cherubim, shadowing this mercy-seat; and that the glory of the Lord God of salvation, dwelling between these cherubim, is the symbol of God's gracious presence; and the non-consuming fiery pillar is but the heavenward elongation of this glorious symbol.

This traveller is every child of Adam—every sinner of his race. The sandy desert is this sinful world. The struggles, trials, afflictions, perils of the way, all represent the painful consequences of sin, which ever meet us here, whilst in an unconverted state: especially the holy law's influences in the conscience, driving us on with its stern commands, and goading to madness and toward despair by its inexorable demand, "*obey and live*;" and yet, at the same time, making it every hour more plain that this just demand transcends the capacity of the sinner—that no pure stream of holy action can emanate from the corrupt fountain of an unholy heart. The wild ranging of the traveller's eye all over the boundless expanse of the desert, in quest of relief, of whose cause he is ignorant, is the sinner crying, in the conscious anguish of his convicted soul, What must I do to be saved? The cloud in the dim distance is the earliest dawn of a confused hope. The fiery pillar, glaring through the darkness, like the star of Bethlehem, tells of a God of mercy and where a clearer light may be found leading to "the Lord our righteousness." Thus too, the moral excellence of the church lures sinners to the ark of safety. "Ye are the light of the world."

Thus our traveller reaches the central point, not simply of the Israelitish camp, but of the moral universe. There is no other principle, known to man, of equal importance with that set forth in this symbol. It gives us the solution of the most important problem ever propounded to the intelligent universe, viz.: How God can justify a sinner. Two other problems, in reference to the fundamental principle of moral government, have been already resolved. This principle is, that righteous action must be rewarded with happiness, and unrighteous action with painful infliction: the one ensures life, the other death. Its application to righteous beings who kept their integrity and their first estate, secured a sentence of justification for the holy angels. This is one problem. Its application to sinning angels, ensured their damnation; this the other problem. Both these are solved. The one resulting in the everlasting life and bliss of the obedient—the righteous; the other in the eternal death of the unrighteous angels that sinned, and who are reserved in everlasting chains, suffering the vengeance of eternal fire. The moral universe had witnessed the adjustment of these two problems: they had witnessed the fate of the righteous and of the wicked. But now there is an intermediate question. Can God be just in justifying a sinner? This question is answered—this problem is solved, by the ark of the testimony, as we have seen in chapters ii., iii., and iv.: but must now, according to promise, make still more manifest.

The ark is the grand type of Christ as the fulfiller of law—of law *preceptive* as contra-distinguished—from law *penal.* It has nothing to do directly with *penalty.* This latter is the precise thing taught by the altar of burnt-offerings; and we must not confuse the symbols. To secure man in the enjoyments of the reward of holy obedience and bring him under the dominion of the law in fact and indeed, include a very large portion of the gospel, viz.: justification and sanctification: the latter is a necessary consequent of the former, and is therefore rather inferred from the symbol meaning of the ark, than expressly taught by it: its grand lesson being Christ's fulfilment of preceptive law for lost men.

The gospel, of which this is the central thought—the master idea, is a *remedial law*, by which "is meant that the scheme of redemption revealed in the Bible, professes to counteract the evils resulting from a former scheme, to make amends for its violation, to provide a remedy for the moral diseases induced through its agency, and so to "heal the hurt of the daughter of my people."

"The evidence may be found in the professed design of the Saviour. He came to fulfil all righteousness—to seek and to save that which was lost, to heal the sick, to cleanse those infected with the leprosy of sin, to rescue man from the condemnation of the law, and to restore him to the favour and enjoyment of God, to throw open the prison doors, and to proclaim liberty to the captives, to give sight to the blind, to make the lame walk, and the tongue of the dumb sing for joy. The entire phraseology of Scripture shows that the gospel is a remedy for evils consequent upon some scheme of law which preceded it. It is not a device original, in and of itself, but is manifestly based upon the hypothesis of another covenant having preceded it, at the head of which is another Adam, of whom this second Adam is the anti-type. The actual work accomplished by the Lord from heaven, is remedial: he restores from the ruin of the fall." See Junkin on Justification, pp. 182, 183.

But now, "every remedial law establishes the principle of the original institute. This is implied in the term by which I have expressed the idea. To speak of remedying a defect, supposes the existence of the thing in which it exists. In human legislation, an original institute defines its object, and the principle by which it proposes to accomplish it. The general law for the establishment of schools in a commonwealth, specifies its object—the education of the entire mass of the people: it also settles the great principle upon which it shall be done. This is an original institute. But many defects may be developed in the application of its detail. These it may be possible to cure, without abandoning either the object or the general principle by which it is proposed to secure it. Subsequent laws may correct the defects, and such laws are *remedial*, and in our legislation are called *supplements*. Should the legislature hereafter determine to abandon the object, or the principle, they must pass a repealing act. But *moral* laws cannot be repealed, even by a divine ordinance. They are an expose of the divine perfections, and are eternal like their author; and hence the reason why the *law* given to Adam, could never be repealed, abrogated or set entirely aside. It is a moral law, and can no more be changed, than God himself, of whose perfections it is a transcript. By a change in man, it has wrought death, and must continue to work death, unless the omniscient Legislator provide a remedy. The law, he can never repeal; a supplement remedial he has revealed in his holy word. The obligation upon Adam and his race, to obey God, as we have seen, never can cease: the motive to obedience, held out in the promise of life, never can be withdrawn. "If thou wilt have life, keep the commandments." The gospel does not make void the law; "God forbid; yea we establish the law." But "what the law could not do, in that it was weak through the flesh—by man's failure—God, sending his own Son, in the likeness of sinful flesh, and for sin, condemned sin in the flesh, that the righteousness of the law might be fulfilled in us, who walk not after the flesh, but after the Spirit." So far, therefore, from the gospel being an original law, defining and fixing its own principles, irrespective of any pre-existing scheme or system of law, it is simply a remedial scheme; designed to confirm, and establish the eternal principles of right, laid down in the law and covenant given by his Creator to man. Material things are subject to mutation. Earth's surface may be the theatre of ten thousand ever shifting dramas, whose last act may be a renovated world, emerging from a deluge of fire. Material suns and systems may be blotted out of existence; but God's law is immutable as his own eternal essence. "Think not that I am come to destroy the law or the prophets: I am not come to destroy, but to fulfil; for verily I say unto you, Till heaven and earth pass, one jot or one tittle shall in no wise pass from the law, till all be fulfilled." It is not denied, that the *law* here includes the Mosaic writings, and the prophets, but it is unquestionably true, that the main substance of the whole, is the *moral law*, which is interspersed throughout the Scriptures." Pp. 183–185.

The gospel, then, is a remedial scheme—it comes to remedy the evils of a broken covenant. Now this is done by establishing the principle of the former—that *life is the just reward of righteousness—happiness and holiness are inseparable.* Jesus came to fulfil all righteousness. Deny this, and the universe is a moral chaos, without a governor; establish it; and all is order, safety and peace; the throne of God no longer totters, but is stable as his own eternal being. This is what the ark teaches: to herald this, all the cherubim spread forth their wings; and, as they fly all abroad, proclaim peace on earth—good-will to man—the fulfilment of law is perfected by the obedience of our ever blessed Surety—the Branch from David's root—" and this is the name whereby he shall be called, THE LORD OUR RIGHTEOUSNESS."

Now, this fulfilment of law—this perfect compliance of our Redeemer with all its preceptive claims, as the title and the only possible title to life eternal, was *vicarious.* It was not wrought out and perfected, this righteousness, to secure his own personal justification and to entitle himself to eternal life;

but for his people. He has life in himself, and his fulfilment of law for his redeemed, is more honourable to the law and more abundantly glorifies it, than could the perfect obedience of the whole race of Adam; yet is it wholly available and passes over to the benefit of all them that believe in his name. Thus they stand complete in him. They are arrayed, not in the righteousness of a man, nor yet of an angel; but, far more glorious, in the "righteousness of God"—"which is through the faith of Christ, the righteousness which is of God by faith." And thus the problem intermediate, is solved. God is just whilst he justifies sinners who believe in Jesus. This central doctrine of Christianity is vindicated, whilst the central principle of the moral universe remains unmoved and immoveable.

CHAPTER XVIII.

Relative Position—The Brazen Altar—The Ark—The Golden Altar.

OUR traveller of the desert, as he approaches the pillar of the cloud, discovers, directly between himself and it, another ascending column, of less elevation and of less uniformity, in regard to its hue and steadiness; sometimes dark; sometimes bright; now upright and evenly; now waving and irregular. As night approaches, its lower part becomes somewhat bright and flickering; and anon he ascertains its base to be the altar of burnt-offerings; and itself the column of smoke ascending from the half consumed sacrifice. He must pass by this altar before he can enter the most holy place and stand in presence of the ark. Faith in the Lamb that was slain, precedes faith in the Lord our Righteousness. When we contemplate the ark, the question arises, how can we put on Christ's righteousness and thus be entitled to eternal life, whilst we are under condemnation and actually dead in sin? Can a man be justified and condemned at the same time? Can he be in both states at once? The relative position of the ark and altar solves this difficulty. The altar must be passed on our way to the ark.

Properly speaking, this is *redemption*—the payment of the demanded price, for the release of the captive soul under sin. The wages of sin is death, and justice demands their payment: there is no evasion—"thou shalt surely die." The veracity of God in this threatening, as well as his justice, call for the infliction of the penalty. This truth is brought home to the sinner's heart, by the Spirit and word of God, working in the conscience "a true sense of sin," and, as the heart knoweth its own bitterness, its first, felt necessity is escape from condemnation and the wrath of God, which it suspends over the sinner's head. Hence the exclamation, "What must I do to be saved?" This has reference to release from the impending curse; not to the necessity of that righteousness to which life positive is promised. Painful endurance and the present dread of its continuance and increase, under the impulsions of self-love, absorb the whole attention and fix it upon the one fearful idea of God's wrath, now ready to burst in upon the soul and sink it into the abyss of endless woe. How can I escape? Is there no deliverance? Must I fall beneath the avenging sword of divine justice? To this agonizing interrogation the blazing altar furnishes the only true response—the only response that glorifies God and saves man—"Yea, his soul draweth near unto the grave, and his life to the destroyers. If there be a messenger with him, an interpreter, to show unto man his (the Messenger's) uprightness: then he is gracious unto him, and saith, Deliver him from going down to the pit; I have found a ransom." Job xxxiii. 22–24: "The Son of man came to give his life a ransom for many," Matt. xx. 28. This ransom-price of redemption, lutron, is prominently exhibited in the brazen Altar. See chap. viii. And this is the one grand design of it, as Paul abundantly declares in Heb. ix. where he proves the inefficiency of the typical sacrifices as a price of redemption for the soul. "But Christ being come a high priest of good things to come, by a greater and more perfect tabernacle, (his own body) not made with hands, that is to say, not of this building; neither by the blood of goats and calves, but by his own blood he entered once into the holy place, having obtained eternal redemption for us," eternal *lutrosis*, that is *release*, deliverance from the curse and condemnation of the law. The root idea of this Greek word, is to *loose*, to untie, unbind, set free from bonds; and in fact, as Webster intimates, our English word is a derivation from it. The assumption always, that the thing to be released was previously bound: and so sinners are under condemnation, bound to endure the just sentence of the law. This is the true notion of *guilt—liability to punishment*—the state and condition of a moral being, on whom judgment unto condemnation has passed; which is the natural estate of all mankind. "He that believeth not is condemned already." Guilt is the bond that binds the sinner to the stake for everlasting burning; which is confessed by the worshipper who "binds the sacrifice with cords, even unto the horns of the altar," Ps. cxviii. 27. Christ our passover who is sacrificed for us—in our place and room; and on our behalf, unties this bond—looses the cords of guilt from the sinner, binds them around himself and "suffers, the just for the unjust, that he might bring us to God." Thus, faith in Jesus Christ, who is both our Priest and sacrifice, secures our release from bonds of guilt—snatches us from hell and the grave; so that "there is therefore now no condemnation to them which are in Christ Jesus:" Rom. viii. 1, and because this change of their legal relations is always accompanied by a consequential change of their moral character and temperament, they "walk not after the flesh but after the Spirit;" and so press by the altar into the holiest of all along with their high priest, and there, having been washed at the laver, are enrobed in the glorious garments of the Saviour's righteousness—that is, are *justified;* and fitted to sit down at the marriage supper of the Lamb. Thus, Justification is that judicial act, whereby God declares the sinner to be possessed in law, of that righteousness, to which eternal life is promised and is therefore justly due; and that this righteousness is from Christ "imputed to the sinner and received by faith alone." This is the teaching of the ark; that of the altar is different, viz. that the sufferings of Christ—his bearing our sins—the pains and sorrows due to them—in his own body on the tree, removes guilt for ever from us; glorifies the divine justice, which, despite the tears and agony and blood and cries of the holy and the just One, held the terrible cup to his parched lips until it was exhausted and he cried, "It is finished." Thus pardon is secured—the forgiveness of sins—the removal of guilt, so that the believing sinner is no longer liable to suffer the punishment of his sins, for they all are blotted out and never can rise in the judgment against him.

This pardon is wholly gratuitous, as *to* the sinner himself, and as *from* Jesus; but it is not gratuitous, as *to* Jesus *from* the Father. It is a pardon "bought with blood divine." The *lutron*—the redemption price which Jesus paid, entitles him to the release of his people from the guilt and ruin of sin. It is no more possible that they should be holden of death and hell and the grave, than that Christ himself should be so holden; against which idea, Peter concludes by a logic which swept about three thousand souls into the fold of the good Shepherd.

Moreover herein is taught most significantly the foundation and superstructure of Christ's intercession. The foundation is laid in the symbol meaning of the altar and the ark, and the intercommunication between them. The former two we have had; the latter now claims our attention. The record we have in detail in chap. xvi. of Lev. The high priest is prohibited, on pain of death from going into the holy of holies, except on one day in the year; "In the seventh month, on the tenth day of the month, ye shall afflict your souls, and do no work at all, whether it be one of your own country, or a stranger that sojourneth among you; for on that day shall the priest make an atonement for you, to cleanse you, that ye may be clean from all your sins before the Lord. It shall be a Sabbath of rest unto you, and ye shall afflict your souls, by a statute for ever," ver. 29, 30, 31. This is the high-day—the great day of atonement. But we must, like Paul, condense Heb. ix. 7. "But into the second went the high priest alone once every year, not without blood, which he offered for himself and for the errors of the people." The sacrifices directed by Moses, were a "young bullock for a sin-offering and a ram for a burnt-offering." "And Aaron shall bring the bullock of the sin-offering, which is for himself, and shall make an atonement for himself, and for his house, and shall kill the bullock of the sin-offering which is for himself. And he shall take a censer full of burning coals from off the altar before the Lord, and his hands full of sweet incense beaten small, and bring it within the vail. And he shall put the incense upon the fire before the Lord, that the cloud of the incense may cover the mercy-seat that is upon the testimony, that he die not; And he shall take of the blood of the bullock, and sprinkle it with his finger upon the mercy-seat eastward; and before the mercy-seat shall he sprinkle of the blood with his finger seven times." Such are the offices for the priesthood themselves. He is commanded to take of the congregation, two kids of the goats, to cast lots for one of them for the Lord and the other falls to the people, for a scapegoat. "Then, after he has offered the bullock, shall he kill the goat of the sin-offering, that is for the people, and bring his blood within the vail, and do with that blood as he did with the blood of the bullock, and sprinkle it upon the mercy-seat, and before the mercy-seat," ver. 15. "And Aaron shall lay both his hands upon the head of the live goat, and confess over him all the iniquities of the children of Israel * * * and the goat shall bear upon him all their iniquities unto a land not inhabited," ver. 21, 22. "In like manner, the bodies of those beasts, whose blood is brought into the sanctuary by the high priest for sin, are burned without the camp; Wherefore Jesus also, that he might santify the people with his own blood, suffered without the gate," Heb. xiii. 11, 12: and Lev. xvi. 27. All the sacrifices and ceremonies of the great day refer to Christ; let us note,

1. The high priest's action in laying aside his splendid garments, Lev. xvi. 4, and arraying himself in the plain linen dress of the common priest, symbolizes the Lord of glory laying aside his robes of eternal light and vailing his divinity in human flesh.

The priest's offering of sacrifices for himself and

his sons is an acknowledgment of their dependence on the great sacrifice offered by the Lord, for the sins of men; and proves that the blood of bulls and of goats cannot wash out sins. Their repetition every year moreover proves their inefficiency, that they "can never take away sins."

3. The offerings of the bullock and ram, and the goat of sin-offering for the people, together with the scape-goat—all these typify Christ as lifting up and removing sin. The two goats are one offering—"a sin-offering," ver. 5. One is slain, and its blood, together with that of the "bullock, is sprinkled upon the altar seven times with his finger, to cleanse," ver. 18, 19; but the live goat carries off—removes the sin. Ver. 22: "And the goat shall bear upon him all their iniquities unto a land not inhabited." "Behold the Lamb of God which *taketh away* the sin of the world." The sufferings of Christ, our High Priest, removes, takes away, and for ever separates sin from the people of his love; so that they can never "come into condemnation, but are passed from death unto life," John v. 24. Therefore,

4. The idea that the sacrifice of Christ was made as truly for the damned in hell as for the saints in glory, must be erroneous. Manifestly, if Christ has taken away the sins—all the sins, (unbelief among the rest,) of all men, all men must go to heaven; or then we have the horrible conception of men going down to eternal death, from whom the Saviour, by

his obedience until death, hath taken away all sin! Blasphemous thought!!

5. The connection between the altar and the ark, by the high priest carrying the blood and fire from the altar, through the blue vail into the most holy place, and there sprinkling the blood before and upon the mercy-seat, most beautifully symbolizes the action of our great High Priest. "For Christ is not entered into the holy places made with hands, which are the figures (types) of the true, but into heaven itself, now to appear in the presence of God for us," Heb. ix. 24. "We have an Advocate with the Father, Jesus Christ the righteous: And he is the propitiation (reconciliation) for our sins: and not for ours (Jewish believers) only, but also for the sins of the whole world," 1 John ii. 1, 2. The basis and efficiency of Christ's advocacy is laid in the perfection of his sacrifice. Because "he humbled himself and became obedient until death—even the death of the cross, wherefore also hath God exalted him and given him a name which is above every name," Phil. ii. 8, 9. His exaltation as Mediator, his universal dominion, and the efficiency of his intercession—him the Father heareth always—all depend on and spring from the work done in the days of his humiliation, the centre of whose sorrows is symbolized in the burning altar. But for his payment of the price of redemption, our Advocate has no right to ask the Father for his people's deliverance from the pit in which is no water, or to pray

for the Spirit to be poured out on them. And this suggests

6. The relation of the golden altar to both the ark and the brazen altar. The incense altar, as we have seen, chap. vii., symbolizes Christ as the Intercessor—the Advocate with the Father. It stands immediately in front of the ark, but outside of the vail and in a direct line from the ark to the laver and the brazen altar. No perfume, however, can arise—no pillar of a sweet-smelling odour can ascend, until coals from the outer altar are brought in, and the incense sprinkled on them. The prayer of the wicked is abomination to the Lord. True devotion, real heart-prayer starts out from Gethsemane and Calvary. "And they shall look upon me whom they have pierced, and they shall mourn for him"—then the Spirit of grace and supplications flows forth, the incense burns brightly upon the altar of the heart, and the cloud thereof arises between the cherubim, where God meets with his people for blessing. The poet of nature may talk of kindling his devotion at the stars, but one star alone is adequate to such a flame—the Star of Bethlehem—a spark from the altar that consumes our great Sacrifice.

CHAPTER XIX.

Relative Positions—The Laver—The Candlestick—The Table.

THE laver, see chap. ix., is the type of our Redeemer as the purifier of the church. But this function of his office he accomplishes by the agency of the Holy Ghost, who regenerates the souls of the Lord's purchased inheritance, and carries them onward in holiness for ever. Its position is directly in front of the door of the tabernacle and between it and the altar of burnt-offerings. It sets forth "the washing of regeneration and renewing of the Holy Ghost," Tit. iii. 5. The use of it, as of the whole tabernacle and all its furniture, was for the priests exclusively. But this very use is *vicarious*, that is, the priests and Levites officiate in their services for and on behalf of the people. An Israelite brings his lamb or goat to the priests at the altar, who slay and offer it as a sacrifice: it is the worshipper, not the priest, who confesses his sin and his hope of acceptance, pardon, and peace through the Lamb of God. So the priests wash at the laver before they proceed in the work at the altar; all this is *vicarious:* and thus throughout; the priests and Levites are the agents as it were; and their outward actions are the acts of the people who present the offerings. The believing Hebrew, by his bloody offering, expresses his faith in Messiah as the *Priest* and the *Sacrifice;* and also as the Purifier and Sanctifier of his own soul. His desire and object is to go himself into the holy, yea, into the most holy place not made with hands; and he knows that until he "is washed, and sanctified, and justified in the name of the Lord Jesus, and by the Spirit of our God," 1 Cor. vi. 11, such entrance is impossible. The position of the altar and laver make it evident that other method or way of access into the holy and the most holy places, there is none.

In chapter vi. it has, we trust, been made evident that the Candlestick typifies Christ as the Teacher, who teacheth as never man taught: as the Great Prophet, by whom all accurate knowledge of the divine perfections—and especially of the divine *mercy*, is made known to lost men. Its position on the south side of the former apartment—the holy place, which ever stands with open doors, ensures its radiance not only within, but all abroad in front, over the laver, and the altar, and the gate of the court, and far eastward: so that for miles distant, the traveller may behold, and learn from it, the place of sacred service and the way of acceptable approach thereto.

The lighting of the lamps is official service of the priesthood; but whence the fire is taken the record does not expressly teach. Lucifer matches are a modern invention; and we know of no fire perpetually burning on these premises but that on the brazen altar: "The fire upon the altar shall be burning in it; it shall not be put out: the fire shall ever be burning upon the altar; it shall never go out," Lev. vi. 12, 13. It is therefore a necessary inference, that here, as in the consumption of the incense, the altar supplies the fire: and here again we have a beautiful illustration and argument as to the infinite importance of the doctrine of atonement—or rather satisfaction rendered to divine justice by the suffering and death of the Mediator. "Put out" this fire—deny the vicarious nature of Christ's sufferings—maintain that Jesus did not *legally*, as our *Surety*, bear our sins—suffer the *penalty of the law* for his people, and you sweep away the foundation of the sinner's hope for eternity. "Put out" this, and you have no fire to light the lamps that guide the sinner's feet into the holy of holies—you have no fire to kindle the incense of an all prevailing intercession—no Advocate with the Father to present the cries and prayers of a ransomed world, and to sprinkle the memorial of his own blood, as the ground and reason why the Spirit should be sent down to kindle pentecostal fires in the hearts of lost millions. Oh! what do men that minister mean by tampering with this fundamental doctrine? Do they know that they are labouring to extinguish the only fire which can generate the power indispensable to give motion to the entire machinery of gospel grace? Do they mean to turn the Shekinah of glory into a black cloud of divine wrath, soon to burst upon an unredeemed race?

In chap. v. we endeavoured to show that the table and its appurtenances exhibited the Saviour to the faith of his people, as the bread of God which cometh down from heaven and sustaineth the life of God's people. Its position is on the north side of the sanctuary, or first apartment of the tabernacle, and, of course, opposite to the candlestick. The table and all its contents must be viewed as one symbol, just as the candlestick, its oil and light, is one; and the incense with its odour is one. It remains only to show the teaching of its relative position. It is accessible as food only on the Sabbath morning and days following, and is therefore at least a week old before it can be eaten. Is this designed as a dietetic lesson? Does it teach that fresh, warm bread is not wholesome?

This bread is accessible only for the priests, who are the representatives of the people: hence, under the gospel, we, the private members of the kingdom, being admitted to its most sacred privileges, are priests unto God. But mainly, it is accessible only by passing the altar, and the laver, as guided by the Candlestick, under whose light it is eaten. That is, Divine teaching must precede actual feeding upon the bread of God. Knowledge of divine truth precedes spiritual nourishment, and must accompany growth in grace thereby. Before eating, the priest must pass the laver also: *i. e.*, he must be washed, or he cannot eat. Unless he is regenerated and sanctified, he cannot digest this spiritual bread. Food is for living men, and not for the dead. Spiritual bread is for such as are made alive in Christ Jesus: to all others the experience cannot be realized—"My flesh is meat indeed, and my blood is drink indeed." The altar too must be passed. Faith in the great sacrifice precedes the feast upon the bread of faces. The eating is in the *presence* of God, and after the priest has passed the altar, and has had the blood put upon the tip of his right ear, in token of entire obedience to divine teaching; upon the thumb of his right hand, in token of his active service rendered to God; and upon the great toe of his right foot, in token of his following in the footsteps of the Lamb whithersoever he goeth.

From all these, it seems impossible to avoid the inference, in reference to the bread and wine in our sacramental supper, that four things ought to be insisted upon as pre-requisites: viz.,

1. "Knowledge to discern the Lord's body"—an intelligent comprehension of the gospel doctrines.

2. "Faith to feed upon him"—a candid profession of belief in the leading doctrines.

3. "Repentance and love"—a reasonable and Scriptural account of religious experience and heart work.

4. "New obedience"—a life of holiness—ear,

hand, and foot—the entire consecration of the person to God.

Omit any one of these, and you endanger the soul of the communicant and lead him on to eat and drink damnation to himself; and prepare the way for conduct dishonourable to the church; and cast a stumbling-block in the way of others.

Strenuously, but tenderly, sincerely, but kindly, press these four points upon the heart and conscience of enquirers, until they shall have examined themselves; and so let them eat—and you will save the evils mentioned; and a holy, active, and zealous communion will ensure peace and harmony, and love, and power for good to your whole congregation. This will ensure your light to shine forth over the dark deserts of a sinful world, and to direct the weary feet of many a wanderer into the path that shineth more and more unto the perfect day.

CHAPTER XX.

Miscellaneous Suggestive Analogies—The Sojourn of Israel—Bondage in Egypt—Forty Years in the Wilderness—Order of March—Westward Movement—Entrance into Canaan.

THE word *sojourn* describes the state of an individual or company of persons who have removed from their own country and kindred, and are living in a foreign and strange land. "Abraham's sojourn began when he obeyed the Lord's call and left Ur of the Chaldees, because the Lord had said unto him, 'Get thee out of thy country, and from thy kindred, and come into the land which I shall show thee,'" Acts vii. 3. This was in the seventieth year of his life, and A. M. 2078. Thirty years after this Isaac was born; and thus Abraham's seed sojourned four hundred years, Gen. xv. 13; whilst the whole sojourn, from the call, was four hundred and thirty years, Exod. xii. 40, 41, at the end of which, "even the self-same day, it came to pass, that all the hosts of the Lord went out from the land of Egypt." Of these four hundred and thirty, two hundred and twenty were passed at the time of Jacob's descent. From the call to Isaac's birth is thirty, to Jacob's sixty, and to his audience with

Pharaoh one hundred and thirty. So that from this to the exodus was two hundred and ten years—this is the whole period spent in Egypt: and this was the term of Israel's deepest degradation, and yet, very possibly, of their most rapid advancement in numbers and general improvement—perhaps even in spirituality.

How well adapted, all this, to impress upon our minds the truth that we are all pilgrims and strangers sojourning in a foreign land, far away from our Father's house! How long and how painful our subjection to cruelty and oppression, under the bondage of sin and the buffetings of Satan and his task-masters! And yet how perverse and foolish and disobedient we are, to fall in love with our chains, and shrink away from the duty of resisting the adversaries and of breaking loose from our own degradation! Israel in Egypt is an allegory, illustrative of man's servitude until he is delivered by divine power, and borne, almost in opposition to his desire, across the red sea, and witnessed its shores strown with the relicts of a dead tyranny.

But if the bondage sojourn in Egypt is symbolical of man's slavery to sin, the additional forty years' pilgrimage in the wilderness is necessarily suggestive of the sinner's condition after his chains are broken, and before he settles down into a peaceful and quiet frame of mind. The inconveniences, exposures, and sufferings; the windings and turnings, the scorching heats and the chilling blasts, the wild beasts and the poisonous reptiles,—all that is harassing and perilous as to their outward condition, have their counterpart in the uncertainty, the failing of faith, the temptations of the adversary of souls; the blindness and darkness; the fights within and the foes without; the allurements of the world, and all the miseries resulting from those fleshly lusts that war against the soul's peace. All this journey through this great and terrible wilderness symbolizes the religious experiences of the present state, preparatory to our entrance upon the heavenly Canaan. This world is a desert, and through it we must pass. Faith alone can secure us. Manna is provided—heavenly bread: water shall be sure. Twice a miracle was wrought to procure a supply. Here it may be proper to correct a misconstruction of the passage, 1 Cor. x. 4: "And did all drink the same spiritual drink; for they drank of that spiritual Rock that followed them: and that Rock was Christ." Some people suppose that the stream from the rock at Horeb followed literally the Israelites in all their journeyings through the desert. But Paul says nothing like this: he, on the contrary, tells us it was the spiritual ROCK—Christ—not the natural water, that followed them; it was the *spiritual drink* which the believing fathers drank, not the *natural water*. "But with many of them God was not well pleased." The believing people drank the spiritual drink, and the others "were overthrown in the wilderness."

The order of march is a pattern for military movements to this day. The whole adult male population, exclusive of Levi, was divided into *four corps*, as military men would now term it, and each corps into three divisions: each division had its captain and proper standard. The whole number of males "from twenty years old and upward, all that were able to go forth to war in Israel," was 603,550. In camp and on the march they were to occupy their proper position. On the march the camp of Judah led off, with Issachar's and Zebulon's divisions: then followed the second corps, the camp of Reuben, with Simeon's and Gad's. Next to these were the tabernacle and its appurtenances, surrounded by the Levites in established order. Then the camp of Ephraim, with the divisions of Manasseh and Benjamin. The camp of Dan, with the divisions of Asher and Naphtali, forming the fourth corps, closed up the rear.

If only one out of five was qualified for military duty, the whole population, exclusive of Levites, was 3,017,750—three millions, seventeen thousand, seven hundred and fifty; add the Levites, 45,000, and you have the grand total of 3,062,750.

The wisdom that could muster and march this immense host for forty years must be more than human, and of this the proofs abound. The Captain of the Lord's host that appeared to Joshua on the right bank of Jordan was the sleepless guardian of this vast host, Josh. v. 14, 15. And thus it is with the spiritual Israel. Order and beauty reign in the camp where Jehovah dwells. "The king's daughter is all glorious within."

These hosts of the Lord marched to all points of the compass betimes, yet they entered Canaan from the east; and the tabernacle always faced the east: so the worshippers always faced and moved westward in their approach to it. This suggests that evangelical truth travels westward. The Star of Bethlehem came from the east. The Sun of Righteousness follows the course of the natural sun. The true church of God has always been moving "from the rising of the sun to the going down of the same." And the facts of history seem alluded to in the language of prophecy. "As the lightning cometh out of the east and shineth even unto the west, so shall the coming of the Son of Man be," Matt. xxiv. 27. "He shall not fail nor be discouraged till he have set judgment in the earth, and the isles shall wait for his law," Isa. xlii. 4. This is spoken of Messiah, and contains a promise for the *West.* The Hebrews called all western regions to which they went by water, *isles:* and many are the allusions to them. "Sing unto the Lord a new song—ye that go down to the sea, and all that is therein; the *isles* and the inhabitants thereof." "And I will set a sign—to the *isles* afar off, that have not heard my fame."

"Westward the course of empire takes its way;
The four first acts already past,

> A fifth shall close the drama with the day;
> Time's noblest offspring is the last."

Canaan, whither Israel was bound, was given to that people by covenant, promise, and oath: and Canaan is the grand type of heavenly rest for the church. Heaven is given to its redeemed inhabitants that are and shall be, by promise, covenant, and oath. All exhibitions, therefore, which ignore the doctrine of the covenants, and make heaven a mere free-will offering from God, which he may recall and change at pleasure, are radically defective. Jesus is the Surety of a better covenant, established upon better promises." "And I will make an everlasting covenant with you, even the sure mercies of David." Into this beautiful land, thus guaranteed by the promise, covenant, and oath of Him who cannot lie, the children of the covenant are sure to enter. From Pisgah's top the eye of faith traverses the earthly Canaan, type of that other Canaan which lies beyond the Jordan of death. On its farther shore, oh! what crowds of bright spirits stand—all arrayed in the fine linen which is the righteousness of the saints—all bent forward in earnest expectancy of the arrival of some dearly beloved friends from the wilderness of a sorrowful world. When lo! the cold flood parts, the ark descends into the dry channel, closely followed by the hosts of God's redeemed, who soon clasp their now recognized friends in the warm embraces of an everlasting love; and with them scan the heavenly home, and traverse the golden streets of the New Jerusalem: and are ushered into the presence of the Lamb that was slain. And now the symbolical ark, and altar, and tabernacle, and all are gone; the pillar of fire is gone; and the smoking column is gone; and the laver is gone; and the incense altar is gone; and the table of shew-bread is gone; and the golden candlestick is gone; "And I see no temple therein: for the Lord God Almighty and the Lamb are the temple of it. And the city has no need of the sun, neither of the moon, to shine in it: for the glory of God doth lighten it, and the LAMB is the light thereof." "Amen, even so come, Lord Jesus."

Jerusalem, my happy home,
  Name ever dear to me!
When shall my labours have an end,
  In joy, and peace, and thee?

When shall these eyes thy heaven-built walls,
  And pearly gates behold?
Thy bulwarks, with salvation strong
  And streets of shining gold?

O! when, thou city of my God,
  Shall I thy courts ascend,
Where congregations ne'er break up,
  And Sabbaths have no end?

There happier bowers than Eden's bloom,
  Nor sin nor sorrow know:
Blest seats, through rude and stormy scenes,
  I onward press to you.

Why should I shrink at pain and woe,
  Or feel at death, dismay?
I've Canaan's goodly land in view,
  And realms of endless day.

Apostles, martyrs, prophets there
  Around my Saviour stand;
And soon my friends in Christ below,
  Will join the glorious band.

Jerusalem, my happy home,
  My soul still pants for thee;
Then shall my labours have an end,
  When I thy joys shall see.

CHAPTER XXI.

A correction—The vicarious nature of the atonement, and its consequences.

ON page 79, there is a small error, which was not detected in time to correct it, and which affects not the meaning, but only the mechanical accuracy. "These corner boards, facing the east, thus constituted a brace and support to the sides north and south, whilst they became door-jambs, of eighteen inches, leaving the door or gateway into the building ten feet and a-half wide." It ought to be *twenty-seven* inches; that being the width of each board. Of course, the space of the gateway remaining would be *nine feet*, and the four apertures made by the five pillars, and including their diameter, would be but two and a quarter feet, and not "two and a half feet for each of the four doors," as stated at the bottom of the page.

As this little book designs to be expository and didactic, and a kind of compend of Christian theology for practical use, it has purposely avoided any extended remarks on disputed points. But, as the brazen altar is the practical starting-point of all the Jewish worship—as without its perpetual fire, no bloody sacrifice can be offered up; no sweet perfume can arise from the golden censer and float upward, drawing the hearts of the worshippers heavenward; no high priest can enter the holy of holies; no pious heart can unburden itself by laying his hand on his victim's head and there confessing his sin and expressing his faith, that his offering is accepted for him to make atonement for him—as without this fire to generate it, there can be no active force to put the entire machinery in motion—it seems proper to close with a brief vindication of the grand doctrine taught at the flaming altar—the vicarious substitution of the Son of Man in the law-place and room of his redeemed, and his full payment, by his sufferings, of the debt due for their iniquities when "he bare our sins, in his own body, on the tree."

Referring the reader back to Chapters VIII. and XVIII., and assuming that he accepts the exposition, we aver that its results cannot be declined. But, if Christ suffered for us as a vicarious substitute, it must have been because he was such; that is, because he put himself, and the Father appointed him to be, legally in our place, bearing our responsibilities; because he was our surety. On any other supposition than this, it is utterly impossible to account for the fact so fully asserted in Scripture, that he suffered by express appointment of the Father, and to justify that appointment. But, if it be true, that our Lord voluntarily put himself in our law-place and room, so that he became sin [a sin-offering] for us, who (personally) knew no sin, then inevitably must he endure the wrath of God due to us. Accordingly, this cup, put into his hand by the Father, could not be taken away, but must be drunk. This is what we mean by the assertion, that Christ's sufferings were strictly and truly *vicarious*. He took away our sins, the sins of all his redeemed, by the sacrifice of himself; so, that they never can rise and appear in judgment against them. And, if he did not do this—and if, in consequence, their sins will rise in the judgment and condemn them, of course his sufferings did not cleanse them from all sin; Christ died as to them in vain. There is no stopping-place between the vicarious nature of Christ's sufferings and the rejection of his entire salvation. If he did not, as your surety, dear reader, take away your sin, it still lies upon you and will take you away into everlasting burnings.

All this seems exceedingly plain. The perpetual fire kept it for ever before the eye of the Jewish believer. The smoke of the brazen altar incessantly reminded him, that access to the holy of holies—type of the heavenly glory—there is none, but by the blood of sacrifice, not his own blood, but that of the lamb substituted in his place, and accepted to make atonement for him. But the believing Israelite never limited his view to the lamb and the burning altar, and the tabernacle, and the ark. The eye of his faith ascended with the smoke and beheld the Lamb that was slain for him. Nevertheless, and notwithstanding all this, men there are, who deny the vicarious nature of Christ's sufferings and death. They hold and teach, that he did not in any legal and proper sense, suffer the punishment of our sins; that he was not so a surety as to become responsible for his people when they failed; that his sufferings were endured to give an example of patient submission in sorrow and anguish, and were inflicted, as a governmental arrangement, to give an exhibition of public justice. But now, if the design was, to give an example of patience under suffering, and if, as must be the case in their view, his sufferings were not at all of the nature of penal evil and from the curse of God; he utterly failed, for he cried aloud, "My God, my God, why hast thou forsaken me," whilst the culprits on his right hand and his left gave no such semblance of impatience. And as to satisfying public justice, the difficulty is still greater, for how is public justice met? Does public justice call for the execution of innocence? If the infliction of excruciating sufferings and unutterable anguish upon a person confessedly innocent, who never transgressed law himself, and who was in no legal sense responsible for the sins of others—if such infliction is an exhibition of public justice, where, out of hell, or in it, shall we look for an exhibition of public injustice? Oh! how they blaspheme who charge the government of God with such an exhibition of justice! But now, admit the vicarious nature of Christ's death; admit that legally, by imputation, "he, his own self, bare our sins in his own body on the tree," and all is luminous as the shekinah itself. Christ had assumed a suretyship for his redeemed: they failed, and consequently their sins were laid on him, and, therefore, die he or justice must.

Into this more than insane philosophy above controverted, this diabolical justice, men most probably have been driven by two errors of seemingly small importance. First, it is assumed, that at the judgment, no sin but unbelief will be regarded as the ground of damnation. Unbelief, under the gospel, is *the* damning sin. Unbelief *is* the damning sin; not, however, because all other sins are lost sight of and escape the eye of the Omniscient Judge, but precisely the reverse, because unbelief spreads them all out in glaring colours before the dread tribunal. Where faith in Christ is, all the sins of the believer are washed out and can never appear to his condemnation; and, as there is no other fountain adequate to this, he that continues in unbelief, that refuses to wash in this fountain, passes to the judgment with all his sins upon him. This is the obvious reason, why, under the gospel, unbelief is the damning sin.

It has been argued from this erroneous assumption, that the heathen who has never heard the gospel, and who, therefore, could not commit the sin of unbelief, can never be condemned, or at least, with but a very slight condemnation. And this conclusion is logical from the premise. If you admit that unbelief is the only damning sin, and that a knowledge of the gospel is necessary before a man can commit the sin of unbelief, it will follow, that a knowledge of the gospel is necessary to damnation. Hence, would follow the corollary, that to send the gospel to the heathen is a great crime and a sin against charity. Something like this was the ground taken by the earlier agents of Britain, at Calcutta, before and during the mission of Claudius Buchanan; and their position was well taken, if the error we expose is not an error, but a portion of gospel truth.

But the basis of the infidel argument is a glaring falsehood. The gospel is not a necessary instrument indispensable to the damnation of a sinner. These go away into everlasting fire prepared for the devil and his angels, because they have sinned against the laws of God, just as the devil and his angels did, to whom no gospel was ever offered.

The second mischievous error alluded to takes its rise partly from the first, and partly from a misconstruction of certain passages of Scripture. Assuming that some knowledge of the gospel is necessary to work the sinner's condemnation, they are easily led to put this construction, for instance, on Jno. iii. 19: "And this is the condemnation, that light is come into the world, and men loved darkness rather than light, because their deeds were evil." Thus, they ignore the latter clause; they lose sight of the evil deeds and exclude them from all share in procuring condemnation; whereas, they are the very cause of the unbelief which prefers darkness to light. Hence, because men could not be condemned, as they suppose, for unbelief, i. e., for rejecting Christ, unless he had died for them, they infer the atonement must be universal; and then appeal to such general expressions as, "he gave himself a ransom for all;" "he tasted death for every man," "and not for ours only, but also for the sins of the whole world." They do not consider, that in these cases the object is to rebuke the Jews' prejudices and efforts to limit the Messiah's work to the natural seed of Abraham, to the exclusion of the Gentiles, among whom are scattered his spiritual seed. The contrast is between the *natural* and the *spiritual* seed; Christ gave himself for the salvation of us Jews; true, says the Apostle, but also for the salvation of Abraham's children according to the promise, who are spread over the whole world.

It is impossible within our brief space to give here the true explanation of all these general expressions. There is no *general* sacrifice provided at the brazen altar. All sacrifices there are *particular*. The offering of the individual is for himself, "to make atonement *for him*," Lev. i. 4; or, if the head of a family, "for his household," Lev. xvi. "When a ruler hath sinned, the priest shall make an atonement for him," iv. v. 22, 26. So, on the great day of atonement, see Lev. xxiii. 24, &c., "to make an atonement for *you* before the Lord," for the *people* of God, *specifically* and *particularly*, "to make an atonement for Israel," "for all Israel." In short, if the reader will take the trouble of spreading open Cruden's Concordance, at the word *atonement*, he will find that, in all cases wherein the object of the sacrifice, that is, any person or thing for which atonement is to be made, is mentioned, it is *always particular* and *never general.* No sacrifice is set forth for the world at large, for the heathen, for mankind in general, for the lost in hell: no *indefinite atonement* was ever made at the altar of God.

But we are asked, is not the blood of Christ *sufficient* for the salvation of all mankind? We answer, certainly; yea, for ten thousand sinful worlds like ours; and his sufferings and sacrifice would be the same, if only one sinner was designed to be saved by it. Because the penalty of the law is death. So, in human governments, if a hundred men unite in murdering a single person, they are all and every one deserving of death: and, if one man murders a hundred, he alone dies on the gibbet. Why this apparent inequality? Because the penalty for murder is death—the death of the murderer.

It is usual, on this question of the extent of the atonement, to say, "sufficient for all, efficient for the elect;" and on this, to base the general gospel call. The sufficiency, I have just affirmed; but when you make this the basis of the command, "Come unto me all ye that labour, &c.," you change the very nature of his sacrifice and its results; you assume that his death did take away the sins of the non-elect; for how otherwise could it make their sins, and especially their unbelief inexcusable? And this is the very design of the position, "sufficient for all," as you present it. But, if his death took away the sin of unbelief, as I have elsewhere observed, and all the other sins of all men, why are not all saved, and the sentence, "these shall go away into everlasting fire," blotted from the sacred page? No! Christ did not take away and for ever blot out the sins of those in hell, as this argument for general atonement assumes. Nor is this at all the ground of the commands, repent, believe, seek the Lord, &c., &c.

The gospel call is properly analyzed into a *command* and a *promise*. The command emanates from the king's authority; the promise from a brother's love. Accordingly, the evangelical commission is prefaced thus: "All power is given unto me in heaven and in earth; go ye, therefore, &c." Therefore he "commandeth all men everywhere to repent." Acts xvii., 30. Obligation to obey the king's authority is universal, absolute and eternal. Satan is bound by it as much to-day as before he rebelled; and lost men on earth and in hell are equally bound to obey God. And the gospel call is first a command: everywhere it addresses us in that form. "Seek the Lord; turn ye, turn ye; come, take my yoke; repent ye; believe on the Lord."

Moreover, the gospel call is *promissory*. "I will give you rest; ye shall find rest; ye shall be saved; hath everlasting life; shall not see death; shalt be with me in paradise, &c." All these *promises* originate in love; and, what is important for us, none of them is indefinite, but all particular; none of them is absolute, but all conditional. They are all addressed to the believer, the penitent, the obedient who submit to the command-call. To none but these is the promise sure. In this sense, faith and repentance, i. e., holy submission, are conditions of salvation; without them, no man is saved; with them, no man is lost. For, be it well remembered, faith and repentance are here not subjectively taken; not as being our *works;* but, as being graces of the Holy Spirit. The king commands all his subjects to return to due allegiance; he promises life eternal to all who shall and do return; he sends his Spirit, who works out in the soul the necessary conditions; then the promise is sure to the day of final redemption.

Our prime duty and privilege is, to pray for the gift of the Holy Ghost. "If ye, then, being evil, know how to give good gifts to your children, how much more shall your heavenly Father give the Holy Spirit to them that ask him." Luke xi., 13. Amen.

ALPHABETICAL INDEX.

www.ingramcontent.com/pod-product-compliance
Lightning Source LLC
LaVergne TN
LVHW021400110826
845150LV00007B/1724

* 9 7 8 1 4 2 5 5 1 3 9 8 6 *